PROUD TO SERVE

The Voices of the Women of Cumann na nGaedheal and Fine Gael

1922-1992

Maria Hegarty and Martina Murray

FINE GAEL ★

First Published in Ireland in 2021 by Fine Gael,
51 Upper Mount Street Dublin 2, D02 W924, Ireland.

© Fine Gael 2021

All rights reserved. No part of this publication may be reproduced or transmitted in any form or by any means, electronic or mechanical, including photography, recording or any other information storage in a retrieval system without prior permission from the publishers.

ISBN 978-1-9160754-0-5

Designed, printed and bound in Dublin, Ireland by Fine Gael.

To the women who stood up, got elected, their teams and the people in Cumann na nGaedheal and Fine Gael who helped make it happen.

To those women who ran and didn't make it, whose stories are yet to be told.

To the two women who continue to inspire us, our mothers, Myra Hegarty and the late Kaline Murray RIP.

We hope these brief glimpses spark interest and inspire others so that women are written into our political history in this era of centenaries in Ireland.

ACKNOWLEDGEMENTS

First off, our heartfelt thanks to the extraordinary women who inspired the writing of this book. We are indebted to them for their enthusiasm and generosity in sharing their experiences so openly, and for their encouragement in enabling us to gather such valuable first-hand accounts about the contribution that women have made to Irish public life.

Our thanks also to the families and friends of those elected women that we couldn't speak to directly, who helped with fact checks and provided additional background information we would not otherwise have been aware of; Noeleen Smith, Mary McKiernan, Garret Ahearn, Sarah Barnes, Ailbhe Hennessey, Ann Marie Burke Browne, Pól Ó Murchú, Anthony Lawlor, Garrett Fennell, Vincent Blake, Paddy and Mary O'Toole, Cahir O'Higgins and Des Walsh, and to Marjorie Moore who opened up a treasure trove of information to us through an archive of newspapers stretching back over forty years.

Special thanks to Nattanna Meredith, graphic designer extraordinaire whose creative acumen and imaginative vision made this book such a beautiful publication and to Maggie McKenna and Ger McDonnell for all their work to get it into print. Thanks also to Suzanne May whose professional proofreading skills proved invaluable in completing this publication.

We are grateful to the staff of Fine Gael for their unwavering help and support and in particular to Terry Murphy for his assistance with the Party archives and Tom Curran for his vision and leadership. This project is one manifestation of his, and his colleagues' commitment to achieving gender equality in politics.

Thanks also to Maurice Manning and Jim Duffy, experts on the history of the Party, for commenting on the final draft. In addition, we would also like to acknowledge the help of Sinéad McCoole, Maggie Mulhare and the Commemorations Unit, Department of Culture Heritage and the Gaeltacht, and the staff of the National Library of Ireland, UCD Archives, Louth Library Services, and Kilmainham Gaol Museum. Thanks also to Alan Kinsella of Irish Election Literature for his kind help with sourcing election ephemera and images for this publication.

We are eternally grateful to our families and friends for their cheerful encouragement in helping us bring this publication to fruition, in particular to Claire Fitch, Eileen Mageean, Christina McGuckian and Des Hegarty for their valuable assistance with research and practical support.

Any errors or omissions remain the responsibility of the authors. While this publication is not an academic one, we hope it stimulates students of history and politics to study each of these women's legacies, and in so doing further enrich our academic discourse.

CONTENTS

Foreword	2
Introduction	4

1922-1933
Debating The Exercise Of Citizenship For Women

Jane 'Jennie' Wyse Power	13
Eileen (Ellen) Costello	19
Alice Stopford Green	23
Margaret Collins-O'Driscoll	27
Kathleen A. Browne	33
Mary Reynolds	37
Bridget Mary Redmond	41

1957-1979
Shaping The Power Of Politics For Women

Brigid Hogan-O'Higgins	46
Joan Burke	51
Mary Walsh	55
Gemma Hussey	59
Myra Barry	63

1981-1992
Pushing Politics To Deliver Rights For Women

Nuala Fennell	68
Madeleine Taylor-Quinn	73
Mary Flaherty	77
Nora Owen	81
Alice Glenn	85
Deirdre Bolger	89
Katharine Bulbulia	93
Miriam Kearney	97
Patsy Lawlor	100
Monica Barnes	105
Avril Doyle	110
Mary Banotti	115
Theresa Ahearn	119
Helen Keogh	123
Mary Jackman	127
Frances Fitzgerald MEP	131
Bibliography	138
Index	144

FOREWORD

This timely book reminds us that throughout our history there has never been a shortage of women with talent, vision and ambition in Fine Gael and before that, Cumann na nGaedheal. Unfortunately, systematic and cultural barriers meant that talent alone was often not always enough. These twenty-eight stories of female TDs, Senators and MEPs, elected between 1922 and 1992, will both inspire and infuriate. We will be inspired by their courage and devotion to public service, and infuriated by some of the obstacles they faced, and the barriers which prevented other women from getting involved in national politics. I want to congratulate Maria Hegarty and Martina Murray for bringing us the lives of some remarkable women and for providing us with extracts of speeches and interviews so we can hear their own voices.

Role models remind us all that anything is possible. They encourage and inspire us to reach our potential. Reading the stories of these trailblazers will encourage many young people to consider a career in politics, confident in the knowledge that the journey today is a little bit easier because of these women.

From Jennie Wyse Power, who was involved in the Ladies' Land League in the 1880s and became a Senator in the 1920s, to Frances Fitzgerald, our distinguished former Senator, TD, Minister and Tánaiste, and now an MEP, these chapters capture the ideas and values which guided some outstanding figures in our political family.

Some are household names and will be well known to all of us, and we can read about the issues they fought for and the obstacles they overcame. Others are now largely forgotten, and this book rescues them from obscurity and reminds us of their contribution to public life and to making our country a better place.

For me, the book is an eloquent reminder that gender inequality is a deeply ingrained cultural problem and one that has prevented our party, our politics and our parliament from realising their full potential.

It is self-evident we need a culture-change. We need to ensure that all political parties, all organisations, recognise that diversity and broad representation leads to better decision-making and a more productive environment and workplace, whether that's the Oireachtas or elsewhere.

Today one of the hallmarks of Fine Gael has been our leadership on issues of equality and diversity. We are working to lay the foundations to enable true equality of opportunity for all in our society.

In the 2019 European elections, Fine Gael won five seats in the European Parliament, four of them women. Since then, Mairead McGuinness has gone onto become a European Commissioner, the first woman from Fine Gael to hold such an office for Ireland. In the last local elections, 62 women were elected for Fine Gael, more than for any other party.

The General Election of 2020 was very disappointing for Fine Gael generally and also with regard to women's representation. Many outstanding TDs, Senators and candidates were not elected, and among those were many exceptional and able women. There is a lot of work to be done to regain that lost ground, but we will do it. In that, I was pleased to nominate four exceptional women, Regina Doherty, Emer Currie, Aisling Dolan and Mary Seery-Kearney to the Seanad as Fine Gael's four Taoiseach's nominees.

I look forward to the day when 50% of our TDs are women - and that would give future Taoisigh a bigger group of people to select from, and a Government where half the ministers are women.

Having imagined the kind of society we want to live in, we now have to work to achieve it. We can't rely on others to change the status quo, we have to do it ourselves.

This book provides some good examples to guide us along the way.

Leo Varadkar TD,
An Tánaiste and Leader of Fine Gael.
February 2021.

INTRODUCTION

For far too long the work of women in Ireland who sought political office and won has been hidden from our historical narrative. Women have been active in political parties since before the foundation of the state, yet very little is known about female politicians or their achievements. The current era of state centenary celebrations offers a timely opportunity to address this gap, and to hear from those women who served as public representatives both nationally and in Europe.

Proud to Serve uncovers the achievements of twenty-eight women who had successful political careers with Cumann na nGaedheal and Fine Gael. Their voices are presented chronologically by the date of their first election or appointment to the Seanad, Dáil and European Parliament, in the years between 1922 and 1992. These women are critical to the story of Fine Gael. They cast light on the influences and questions of the day, and in the process, not only challenge our understanding of the way politics has been contested and navigated, but also speak to us about what it takes to achieve change.

From Jenny Wyse Power in 1922 to Frances Fitzgerald in 1992, this volume tells us something of the personal and political backgrounds of the women concerned, their motivations for getting involved and their experience of elected life. It also affords us some insight into the issues that were prevalent during their time as public representatives, and their views about the future for women's involvement in politics in Ireland.

The political stories in this volume are told using a combination of original first-hand autobiographical accounts, biographical details and resources from the archives, including excerpts from political speeches, Dáil questions, photographs and election materials. The book is organised chronologically, with individual chapters dedicated to each female politician based on the date of their first election/appointment to the Dáil, Seanad and European Parliament. In remaining faithful to the terminology in use at the time, this approach reveals the evolution of the language around gender equality and women in politics.

The picture that emerges is one of women who were hard working, tenacious and effective politicians. Their service and persistence in the face of the challenges and attitudes they encountered carved out a pathway for women in political life and helped advance the cause of equality for women in Ireland. In bringing together their stories, we hope to generate renewed interest in the contribution and achievements of a remarkable group of women. We also hope to stimulate broader awareness and debate about the role and work of women in Irish political life.

The involvement of women as elected representatives in Irish public life began in 1898 with the enactment of The Local Government (Ireland) Act, which allowed women to vote and run in district council elections for the first time. A year later, eighty-five women were elected as Poor Law Guardians, and thirty-one became Rural District Councillors. Over the course of the next three decades women were also active in forging the foundations of the new political parties that would come to dominate the Irish political landscape in the early twentieth century. Women were involved in helping found the Cumann na nGaedheal organisation, in some cases adopting senior roles. The party that ultimately became Fine Gael emerged out of a number of political groups including Cumann na Saoirse, the organisation established by those women who supported the terms of the Treaty.

The bravery of the women who stood for election in the early years cannot be underestimated. Eileen Costello for instance, who became a senator in 1922, recalled; *"the reason I took the position of Chairman of Tuam Town Commissioners was that men in such positions at the time were liable to be ill-treated or even murdered. I thought they would hardly shoot a woman, and in that way, I could do my bit to help."* Her stance offers a glimpse of the challenging climate then in vogue and reveals something of the spirit of the women engaged in the tumultuous political scene of the time.

The 1922 Free State Constitution confirmed the right to vote for women at twenty-one, on equal terms with men. However, any optimism this may have engendered quickly dissipated. The women who helped to establish an independent Ireland, who had campaigned and battled alongside their male counterparts for freedom and equality, were shocked by the hasty enactment of a series of gender-regressive legislative measures. This retrenchment to traditional attitudes about women's role in the early years of the State copper-fastened a view that women had no place in public life. Moreover, legislative acts and influential papal encyclicals confining the sphere of women to 'life within the home' ultimately found expression in the 1937 Constitution, the consequences of which we are still unravelling today.

In seeking to commemorate the work of women involved in Fine Gael and its precursor Cumann na nGaedheal, we wondered what happened next. What was the experience like for the Party's first female politicians who took their seats in the chambers of Dáil Éireann, Seanad Éireann, and who represented their country in the European Parliament? What do they have to tell us about the prospects for women in politics now and in the future?

The women in this volume refused to be stifled by the social mores and conventions of the time. Deeply embedded in their local communities, the women who joined Fine Gael and its forerunner Cumann na nGaedheal occupied many roles in the Ireland of their time: political activists, suffragists, nationalists, folklorists, farmers, nurses, publicans, chemists, historians, shopkeepers, social workers, wives, mothers, foster parents. In refusing to be confined by the restrictions being placed on the role of women in society, they navigated male-dominated pathways to stand up and run successful election campaigns so that they could represent the interests of their constituents, and, despite their different perspectives in some cases, join the fight for women's equality.

Their stories are fascinating. Jennie Wyse Power, the first woman in this volume, was a member of the Ladies' Land League in the 1880s. In 1916 the Easter Proclamation was signed in her house on Henry Street. She went on to become Vice-President of Cumann na nGaedheal and was appointed a Senator by W. T. Cosgrave in 1922. After she left the Party in late 1925 she was succeeded as Vice-President by Margaret Collins-O'Driscoll, the first female TD elected for Cumann na nGaedheal.

In 1932 Mary Reynolds dutifully took up the mantle when her husband was fatally shot while canvassing for Cumann na nGaedheal during the general election campaign. This cannot have been an easy task. On top of an already tragic situation which left her facing the daunting prospect of raising seven young children, in addition to running a business, she stepped up. The general election was postponed for two weeks in Leitrim-Sligo while the rest of the country went to the polls. The bereaved Mrs Reynolds buried her husband, successfully contested the election and joined her colleague Margaret Collins-O'Driscoll on the Government benches in the Dáil.

Bridget Redmond and Joan Burke too contested elections following the deaths of their husbands. Bridget Redmond secured the seat previously held by her late husband in Waterford at the general election of 1933, while Joan Burke was persuaded by the Party elders to contest the Roscommon by-election two months after her husband's sudden death in 1964. It is worth noting that all three performed consistently well in subsequent elections. While Mary Reynolds lost her seat in 1933, her re-election in 1937 was followed by success in every other election in which she stood until her retirement in 1961. Bridget Redmond continued to hold her seat in Waterford until her untimely death in 1952, while Joan Burke had the enviable distinction of topping the poll in Roscommon in every election she contested, from 1964 until she retired from politics in 1981.

Despite such outstanding electoral success across a number of decades, the idea persists that women were only elected because they were the wives, sisters or daughters of male politicians. As Madeleine Taylor-Quinn notes, *"There is a very selective misconception out there in relation to being handed the seat. Nobody would have referred to Garret Fitzgerald being handed a seat, yet his father was there before him. You don't get a seat without fighting for it."* Indeed, for many of those first elected to national politics in the 1970s and 1980s, the gateway to public life came via a variety of routes, including activism in their local communities and the Women's Rights Movement.

As part of a concerted effort to *"unleash the political potential of women"* under the leadership of Garret Fitzgerald, the Party approached women including Gemma Hussey and Frances Fitzgerald who had already established good public profiles in their own right, to stand for election. In recalling the influence of Garret Fitzgerald, Miriam Kearney notes that he was, *"probably a feminist well before many of his male contemporaries would have understood that term"*, while Katharine Bulbulia observes; *"There was nobody more encouraging. I still have a book where he wrote in the flyleaf, 'Don't let the men get you down'."*

The personal testimonies presented here also reveal a range of motivations for getting involved in political life. Gemma Hussey was inspired by the women's movement and *"a strong belief in liberal politics."* Myra Barry *"strongly believed in the need for a just and caring society"*, while Mary Flaherty was spurred on by her anger at the giveaway budget that wiped out the 1973-1977 Fine Gael-Labour Government that had begun the transformation of Irish society, particularly for women. Meanwhile the well-travelled Mary Banotti attributed her motivation to her experiences while living abroad, as well as to her origins in a family possessed of a strong political history.

Many of those we talked to traced their initial interest in politics back to the views they were exposed to in their early family life. Deirdre Bolger noted the prevalence of political discussion in her house growing up, recalling the visits of Fine Gael leader James Dillon, who was a friend of her father. Mary Jackman's background featured those who were very strong Fine Gael supporters on her father's side coupled with those she describes as *"roaring Fianna Fáil"* on her mother's side, no doubt making for lively debates at family gatherings over the years.

At a time when politics was dominated by the dynastic factor, Myra Barry regarded Young Fine Gael as critical in encouraging people who were not from political families to get involved in politics for the first time. Future TDs and Senators such as Mary Flaherty, Madeleine Taylor-Quinn and Miriam Kearney were all members of Young Fine Gael and some were instrumental in setting up local branches of the organisation in areas that, up to then, hadn't been regarded as particularly fertile recruiting grounds for the Party. Myra Barry and Mary Flaherty were both involved in setting up a branch in Finglas at a time when Labour and Fianna Fáil were the dominant parties there, while Madeleine Taylor-Quinn set up two branches, the first in her native Kilrush and the second in UCG, during her tenure as a student there.

Many of those we interviewed for this publication remarked on how unusual it was to see other women during their time in politics. Katharine Bulbulia describes being *"like a rare bird"* attending meetings of Waterford County Council in the late seventies and early eighties, while Mary Jackman remembered the great welcome she received when canvassing for votes on the Seanad election trail. Her impression was that people *"loved to see a woman coming, maybe because women were rare at that time."* Avril Doyle observed that there had been no female minister in the Department of the Environment before she was appointed. Myra Barry reflects on being one of only eight women in the Dáil in 1979, while Gemma Hussey was the sole woman in Cabinet throughout the five-year period from 1982 to 1987.

Precisely because of their small numbers, many of the female politicians we spoke to were keenly aware of their significance as political role models for other women. As Helen Keogh notes, *"women should be empowered and should be a vital part of society."* While not solely defined by their gender, they rarely ignored gender in their work. Unlike their male counterparts these elected representatives absorbed and represented the relational, multi-dimensional nature of life lived in many spaces – home, community, parliament. This grounded their work in elected office. What's more, it determined the issues they paid attention to including: the lack of equal access to public service jobs, removing the status of illegitimacy, equal access to education for girls, criminalising marital rape, the provision of refuge services for women, access to contraception, pensions for women, children's rights, marriage equality and abortion rights.

These women also succeeded as politicians in doing things in a different way. Having already forged good working relationships through groups such as the Women's Political Association and Women Elect, an organisation set up by Monica Barnes, women were prepared to work across party lines. Many of those we spoke to expressed a general dislike of the adversarial nature of the Dáil, finding the committee system a much more constructive way of performing the business of politics. Referring to her time as Minister for Education, Gemma

Hussey describes making a pact with Mary O'Rourke, her opposite number in Fianna Fáil, prompted by the realisation that *"if we started shouting at each other in the Dáil we would be immediately labelled 'harridans', so we made a pact that we wouldn't get trapped by that kind of thing."*

It is clear from the testimonies of those involved that there were many obstacles for women to overcome, both in getting elected and then in going about their work as legislators. Women were often treated as invisible, while their contributions at meetings were frequently ignored. Frances Fitzgerald articulates a common experience; *"I might say something at Cabinet or at the Parliamentary Party. Some man would say the same thing. The Chair or another man would then quote what a man said, never referencing what a woman said."* Nora Owen observes that in the face of such attitudes women had to be quite assertive, noting that, *"as a minority in the room you had to make sure you got heard."* This appears to have been a regular feature of the so-called 'cut and thrust' of political life for women.

Notwithstanding their small numbers, the breakthroughs they achieved clearly demonstrate the impact women can and do have in public life. In the absence of women such as the pioneering Nuala Fennell, one wonders, how would equality for women have been advanced? It is worth noting that most of the women featured in this volume have been the 'first woman' elected to party, local council, Dáil, Seanad and European political institutions. While each of these 'firsts' is noteworthy, Frances Fitzgerald sounds a cautionary note. The fact is that gender balance is still far from attained. We need more women to run for election.

This volume gives voice to the experiences of an extraordinary group of women, each of whom made important contributions to Irish politics, and balanced many demands at a time when women's participation in public life was particularly challenging. They have ensured that women's rights and gender equality remain a priority for their party. In celebrating their stories, we celebrate all women whose efforts have, and continue to, define Fine Gael. Indeed, their legacy behoves us all, women and men, to strive for further diversity in public life, so that inclusion encompasses more than gender.

These women's experiences ask those of us in this generation to consider what we do now to end, as Monica Barnes challenged in her day, the *"sterility of single-sex politics."* The title of this volume is drawn from views expressed by the women themselves, each of whom talks about how honoured they were to represent their constituents, the pride they took in carrying out their duties in public life, and their gratitude at being given the opportunity to do so. Each of them was proud to serve.

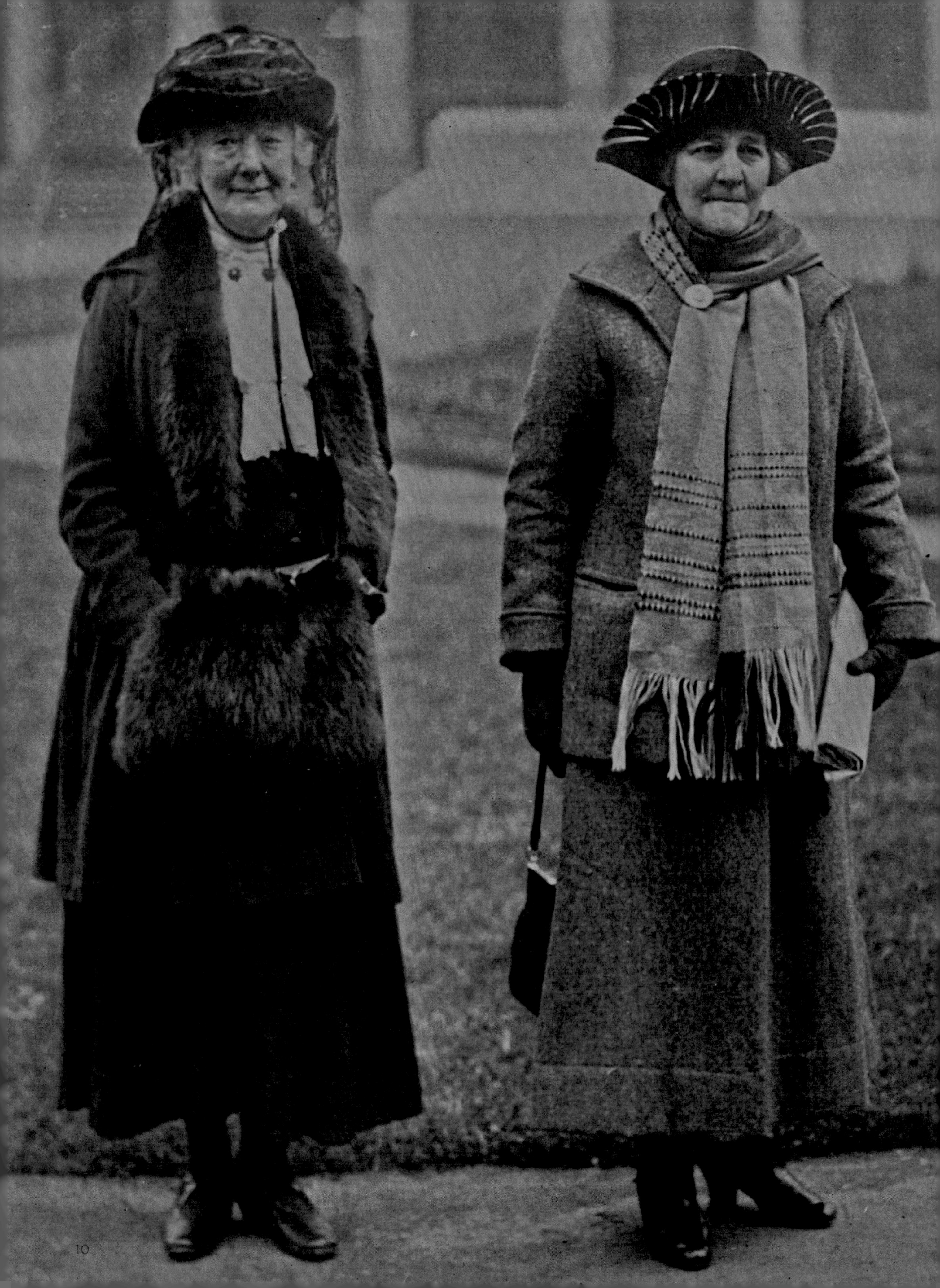

1922-1933
Debating The Exercise of Citizenship For Women

opposite page
Mrs Stopford Green and Mrs Costello, 1922
Courtesy of Bibliotèque Nationale de France

PROUD TO SERVE: The Voices of the Women of Cumann na nGaedheal and Fine Gael 1922-1992

> "If this sex discrimination is to be made by a male Executive Council and by practically a male Dáil I think it very unjust. No consultation of any kind took place with any representative women on the subject."

1922 SENATOR
Jane 'Jennie' Wyse Power

Senator 1922-1936

Founder of Cumann na mBan and Cumann na Saoirse

First female Vice-President of Cumann na nGaedheal

Executive Committee Member Ladies' Land League

Jane 'Jennie' Wyse Power (née O'Toole) began life as a political activist by joining the pioneering Ladies' Land League in 1881. The organisation was the first to actively engage women in organised political activity in Ireland, and Jennie's involvement proved a precursor to her future role as a driving force in many of the country's most significant political movements. Her activities on behalf of the League included working as an organiser in her native Wicklow and Carlow, serving as a member of the National Executive and acting as librarian to the male leaders of the Irish National Land League during their imprisonment in Kilmainham Gaol. Following the acrimonious dissolution of the organisation Jennie succeeded in maintaining friendships with both Anna and Charles Stewart Parnell, and in 1892 published *Words of the Dead Chief,* a collection of excerpts from Parnell's speeches.

Jennie met and married journalist, IRB member and Gaelic Athletic Association founder, John Wyse Power and the couple had four children. The family moved to Dublin where Jennie opened a restaurant and shop on Henry Street. The Irish Farm Produce Shop promoted the work of the Irish artisan food producers of the day, and the business proved so successful that Jennie opened two further branches in Rathmines and Upper Leeson Street. The Wyse Powers also immersed themselves in the cultural revival movement of the time. They joined the Gaelic League and spent many enjoyable holidays in the Ring Gaeltacht area of Waterford, where Jennie subsequently founded an Irish college.

Jennie remained an active participant in political activities throughout the early 1900s. She was a vice-president of Maud Gonne's Inghinidhe na hÉireann and also helped found the Irish Women's Franchise League, Cumann na mBan and later Sinn Féin. Her Henry Street restaurant became a regular haunt for the city's political activists, and it was there that the leaders of the 1916 Easter Rising gathered to sign the Proclamation ahead of its

opposite page
Jane 'Jennie' Wyse Power
Courtesy of Kilmainham Gaol Museum
Ref: KMGLM 2015.0673

inaugural reading at the nearby GPO. Throughout that seminal week, Jennie supplied food to the rebels, until her shop was eventually destroyed by fire. She subsequently provided aid to the families of Republican prisoners and later served as a Judge in the North Dublin Courts. First elected to Dublin Corporation in 1920, her support for the Treaty resulted in her resignation from Cumann na mBan. She then founded the pro-Treaty women's organisation Cumann na Saoirse and served on its executive committee.

In 1922 she was one of four women appointed to the first Seanad by W. T. Cosgrave, and in the early years of the Irish Free State, she proved a vocal advocate of equality for women. She spoke out against the most regressive aspects of legislation undermining the role of women in Irish public life, continually reminding her male colleagues of the vital role women had played in forging the new Irish state, as illustrated in the following excerpt taken from her contribution on the Civil Service Regulation (Amendment) Bill Second Stage 17th December 1925;

> "No men in a fight for freedom ever had such loyal co-operation from their women as the men who compose the present Executive Council. When they wanted messengers to go into dangerous places they did not call on members of their own sex. When they wanted auditors to go out when the old Local Government Board broke down it was women they sent. It was women inspectors that went round through all the Unions and did all the work for them in that terrible time when the whole British organisation practically ceased to operate, and these are the people who tell us that we are physically unfit."

Jennie became the first female Vice-President of Cumann na nGaedheal in 1923, but soon found herself at odds with the Party on a number of issues. She was increasingly disillusioned with the Party's attitude on the Boundary Commission, the Northern question, and citizenship rights for women. The veteran women's rights advocate eventually parted ways with Cumann na nGaedheal following the debate on the 1925 Juries Act. The Act sought to prevent women serving on juries, a fundamental breach of the rights of women to be equal citizens, which had been enshrined in the Irish Proclamation, and guaranteed in the 1922 Constitution. Jennie Wyse Power attended her last meeting as a Cumann na nGaedheal representative in 1925 and, as an independent senator throughout the 1920s and '30s, continued to speak out against further attempts to introduce economic and gender regressive legislation. She later became a member of Fianna Fáil and represented the party in the Senate until its dissolution in 1936. Jennie died at the age of eighty-two in 1941.

> "No men in a fight for freedom ever had such loyal co-operation from their women as the men who compose the present Executive Council."

Cumann na Saoirse

POINTS FOR CANVASSERS

The Treaty rids us of—

(1) The British Army, the instrument of British power in Ireland.
(2) A police force trained for political espionage.
(3) British control of education, which was killing the Irish language and destroying the soul of the nation.
(4) British legislation.
(5) British officialdom which ran the Government of Ireland for the benefit of England.
(6) British control of our purse, and British taxation which left Ireland the one country in Europe with a decreasing population.
(7) The stranglehold of Britain on Irish trade and industry.

The Treaty gives us—

(1) An Irish Regular Army, with modern equipment, sworn to the service of Ireland.
(2) An Irish Police Force designed solely for the maintenance of law and order.
(3) Irish control of education, with power to restore the language and build up a national culture.
(4) An Irish Parliament with full power to make laws and subject to **NO** British veto.
(5) An Irish Executive subject only to the authority of the Irish Parliament.
(6) Power to develop the resources and industries of Ireland, and to stop the drain of emigration.
(7) The raising and spending of our own revenue.

MAHON'S PRINTING WORKS, DUBLIN.

Cumann na Saoirse "Points for Canvassers", 1922
Courtesy of Alan Kinsella, Irish Election Literature

During her time as a Senator Jennie Wyse Power spoke out against many aspects of legislation undermining the role of women in Irish public life, as demonstrated in this excerpt from her speech opposing the Juries Bill of 1927.

30 March 1927

Juries Bill 1927 Second Stage

There is little for me to say at this particular stage except to protest as strongly as I can, and my protest is entirely influenced by the fact that if this Bill becomes law the civic spirit that is developing in women will be arrested. In fact the suggestion that there shall be only male jurors in the future cuts at the very root of this development of the awakening of the civic spirit. We all know that in the past this spirit had been repressed and became stunted and did not grow.

But by the happenings, political happenings if you like, during the last 50 years the men who led political movements and carried them in the main to success, utilised women in order to achieve their object. That utilisation of women helped in a great degree their civic spirit, and some of them, encouraged more or less by the way they have been thrust out, as it were, to do work that they never did before, came gradually into public life and have done social work which is generally regarded as successful.

It is for that reason I deplore so much the Minister's attitude in this matter, not so much, perhaps, because we want to be on juries, or anything else, but because he is doing such an injustice to what is really a necessary asset to every State, the co-operation of its men and women.

The Minister by a bold stroke eliminated females from the panel. Sir James Craig—I am sure in a kindly spirit, I will not say anything else— put down in the Dáil an amendment giving women the right to ask for the privilege of being jurors. I give him all credit for his kindly spirit, but I think it would have been better, before he put down that amendment, if he had a little consultation with those who certainly knew better than he did that that amendment was entirely wrong, and that by it he was about to place a burden on women that perhaps he did not understand. Sir James Craig having been shown this side of the question, became very angry and threw up his hands in despair. He said: *"Absolutely nothing will please you. I am like the old man and the ass."* When he was angry, I am sorry to say, he made the statement I am about to read to you. He said: *"That was not the reason why I put it forward. I said that between the ages of 20 and 40 the majority of women have a much more important duty to perform to the State than serving on juries, that their functions were motherhood and looking after their families, and they objected to these other women who have missed these functions and who wanted to drive to serve on juries those who have something else to do."* Only that Sir James Craig was angry, and very angry, I do not think he would have made that statement. None of the newspapers reported that, but the morning after the debate one of them set out to make a column of merriment of it for its readers. I commend the Deputy in his hour of need to the women voters of Trinity College. I think the Minister knew the material he had when he accepted this amendment. Naturally, Deputies were anxious to vote for anything rather than the total elimination of women. For proof of that I will read what one Deputy said: "*This is the movement of a truculent minority, and this proposed amendment gives us a means out.*" The "*means out*" was a voluntary panel. The proposal was carried by 39 votes to 11. There were 50 votes in all. One wonders where were the other 50 Deputies. All who have thought out this question and who have given consideration to cases where women may be in the dock have come to the conclusion that it is right and proper that a proportion of women should be on juries in such cases. In the Dáil no consideration was given to that question. I think there is a general feeling in the country that in cases where women are concerned a proportion of the jury should consist of women. If consideration had been given to that point I do not think Deputy Sir James Craig's amendment, as embodied in the Minister's Bill, would be carried, because we know that out of that panel you will not get a sufficient number to serve on mixed juries. Some play was made here to-day about the personnel of these associations being similar. I may be active on one association, but I am only on the one. I am sure Senators received a copy of a resolution passed at a meeting of the Dublin Christian Citizens' Council, the Dean of Christ Church being in the chair, in connection with this Bill. The resolution was proposed by Rev. Sinclair Stephenson. I do not think the personnel of that Association can be cavilled at. While I cannot do anything at this stage I do not think I could do less than protest against the motion.

PROUD TO SERVE: The Voices of the Women of Cumann na nGaedheal and Fine Gael 1922-1992

General Election.—Mr. Batt O'Connor, Co. Dublin Cumann na nGaedheal candidate, in conference with helpers touching the final "push." Mrs. Blythe is third from right.—*Irish Independent* Photo (R.).

Courtesy of the National Library of Ireland

1922–1933 Debating The Exercise of Citizenship For Women

> "I believe the Ministers maintain that for some posts women are unsuitable. I rather think the word that should be used is 'unwanted'."

1922 SENATOR
Eileen (Ellen) Costello

Senator 1922–1934

First woman elected to Tuam Town Commissioners

First female chairman of Tuam Town Commissioners 1921–1922

Judge of the Republican Courts

Executive Committee Member of Cumann na Saoirse

Born Edith Drury at Strand Union Workhouse, St Pancras, London in 1870, Eileen Costello trained as a schoolteacher and became head of St Michael's Church of England School in Buckingham Palace Road. In 1896 she joined the Irish Literary Society and the London Gaelic League, where she learned to speak Irish and developed a fluency in the language. Her involvement on the committees of both organisations led her to form friendships with *"the misses Yeats, WB their brother"* and various other figures who populated the London-Irish literary and cultural scene at that time. She was the only woman on the committee of the London Gaelic League and in May 1902 she travelled to Dublin to represent the branch at the organisation's annual Ard Fheis.

That same year she also converted to Catholicism, a decision which meant that she had to resign her position as Head Teacher at St Michael's. She moved to the West of Ireland and secured a teaching position at the Presentation Convent in Tuam. A year later she married fellow Gaelic League member Dr Thomas Bodkin Costello. The couple settled in Tuam and had one child, the writer Nuala Costello. A committed folklorist, Eileen continued to collect traditional Irish folk songs, a practice she first began in London. She later recalled, *"My husband was the local Medical Officer and I went with him on his round amongst the country people, whom he knew very well. They sang the songs and I wrote down the words and music. I did this work in my spare time, which was not easy – being a doctor's wife having to deal with many calls by day and night."* The collection was published in 1919 under the title *Amhráin Muighe Seola: Traditional folk-songs from Galway and Mayo.*

At the invitation of her friend Arthur Griffith she attended a Sinn Féin meeting at the Rotunda in Dublin and, in 1905, she was involved in founding Coláiste Connacht, also known as Tourmakeady Irish College, where other committee members included Douglas Hyde. Meetings of the Irish colleges

Mrs Costello, 1922
Courtesy of Bibliotèque Nationale de France

were periodically held in Dublin, and when the committee secretary Fr Creehan was unable to attend the one scheduled for Easter Saturday 1916, he asked Eileen to attend in his place. She travelled to Dublin and when some business items were held over for conclusion after the Easter break, decided to stay on over the weekend at The Gresham Hotel in Dublin. That Easter Monday, while visiting her mother-in-law who lived on Haddington Road, she learned about events at the GPO. Leaving her daughter, she made her way back across the city to The Gresham where her refusal to contribute to a collection being taken up for two snipers positioned on the hotel roof made her very unpopular amongst the other guests. *"Are you asking me to reward these Englishmen who are shooting our own men down? Have some sense of proportion. I won't give you a penny. You should be ashamed for asking it."* She later reflected; *"My sympathies always were with Ireland in her struggle for independence".* Her account of the events that took place that day was recorded in a witness statement given to the Bureau of Military History in 1955.

In 1920 Eileen Costello was elected the first woman member of Tuam Town Commissioners, and served as its first female Chairman from 1921 – 1922. She later observed; *"The reason I took the position of Chairman of Tuam Town Commissioners was that men in such positions at the time were liable to be ill-treated or even murdered. I thought they would hardly shoot a woman and in that way I could do my bit to help."* She was active during the War of Independence in Tuam where her home was a safe-house and remembered, *"a woman telling me to be careful about a light in a spare bedroom in my house where boys on the run occasionally slept. They had to go to bed in the dark after that."* Austin Stack nominated her as a judge of the Sinn Féin courts, where *"being the only woman I generally occupied the Chair."* After the Civil War Eileen took the pro-Treaty side, and joined Cumann na Saoirse, where she served as a member of the executive committee alongside women including Jennie Wyse Power and Kathleen Browne.

Eileen was one of four women appointed to the Seanad in 1922, where she supported Jennie Wyse Power in speaking against the Civil Service Regulation Bill, confining certain jobs to specific sexes. She was also vociferous in her opposition to the Juries Bill of 1927 requiring women to volunteer for jury service, rather than it being an automatic duty of citizenship as for men. She expressed the view that; *"As we have the vote, and have been given privileges, we should also obey the obligations. I think if women are to take their part as citizens, these duties should be put upon them and enforced, because that is the only way they can be educated into good citizenship."* She served in the Seanad for twelve years, until she lost her seat in the Seanad election of 1934. Eileen died in 1962.

> *"The reason I took the position of Chairman of Tuam Town Commissioners was that men in such positions at the time were liable to be ill-treated or even murdered. I thought they would hardly shoot a woman and in that way I could do my bit to help."*

During her time as a Senator Eileen Costello resisted attempts to restrict the role of women in Irish public life, including the following excerpt from a speech in 1925, where she opposed measures to restrict the employment of women in the Civil Service.

17 December 1925
Civil Service Regulation (Amendment) Bill 1925 (Second Stage)

I would just like to quote from the Constitution Article III., which says:—

"Every person, without distinction of sex, domiciled in the area of the jurisdiction of Saorstát Eireann, ... is a citizen of the Irish Free State (Saorstát Eireann), and shall, within the limits of the jurisdiction, ... enjoy the privileges and be subject to the obligations of such citizenship."

Of course, I am aware that the Constitution can be altered or changed if the alteration or change does not infringe the terms of the Treaty. But, I think, the bringing in of this Bill by the Government is unjust, that it is morally wrong, and I think it is monstrously unfair. The women are still to be subject to the obligation of citizenship, but their privileges are to be curtailed and restricted. I think the qualifications for the various posts in the Civil Service are quite sufficient already. These are the qualifications as to age, health, character and ability, and I do not think any other qualifications are needed. I admit that it is to a certain extent the fault of the women themselves that such a thing as this should be allowed. They had very high privileges conferred on them, but they have not lived up to these privileges. This has been shown during the recent Seanad elections and at other elections as well. I do hope that if actions such as the present one in bringing in this Bill are continued, that the women will very soon wake up. The explanation is that they have not realised their power as yet. That does not apply to Ireland only. It applies to England and other countries in the same way. I really do not understand why this Bill has been brought in. Does it mean that there has been such a rush of women for the various posts that the Government finds it necessary to bring in this Bill? I have not heard anything about such a rush. I believe the Ministers maintain that for some posts women are unsuitable. I rather think the word that should be used is *"unwanted."* They are synonymous terms in the mind of the Minister. It is on the general principle that I object, and I shall vote against the Bill. I see that in England posts, too numerous to mention, are open to women, and very highly paid posts too. I fail to see why restrictions should be put upon them here.

Alice Stopford Green
Courtesy of the National Library of Ireland

1922–1933 Debating The Exercise of Citizenship For Women

> "To Ireland we have given our faith. In Ireland is our hope."

1922 SENATOR
Alice Stopford Green

Senator 1922–1929

One of the Founder Members of Cumann na nGaedheal

Member of Cumann na Saoirse

Prominent in organising Lá na mBan in 1916

One of four women members of the first Seanad in 1922, historian Alice Stopford Green was born in Kells, Co. Meath in 1847.

A committed nationalist, she was involved in preparations for the 1914 Howth Gun Running from her home in London, and provided funding for the venture. In the aftermath of the Easter Rising in 1916 she campaigned in vain to save the life of her friend Roger Casement and later, in her early seventies, moved to Dublin. When the British Government attempted to impose conscription in Ireland, Alice Stopford Green was prominent in organising *"Lá na mBan"*, a day of mass national protests involving tens of thousands of women which took place on 9th June, 1918. Her home at 90 St Stephen's Green quickly became a centre of intellectual activities and Michael Collins was amongst the regular visitors there. She was a strong supporter of the Treaty he helped broker, joining the executive of Cumann na Saoirse, and was later one of the founder members of Cumann na nGaedheal.

At the time of her election as a Senator in 1922, Alice Stopford Green was seventy-five years old, and her declining health meant that she was unable to participate as fully in the life of that institution as she might have wished. Her Seanad contributions chiefly related to matters of history and culture, and she served on a committee to set out a scheme for the editing, indexing and publication of Irish manuscripts. In 1924 she gifted a specially commissioned casket to the Senate to serve as a witness in later times to that institution's *"increasing service to the country."*

Before entering representative politics Alice had a long career as a historian. Her first work, *A History of Henry the Second,* was published in 1888 under her married name, Mrs J. R. Green. She later turned her historical lens to the subject of Ireland, and in 1908 completed *The Making of Ireland and its Undoing.* Her approach challenged the traditional portrayal of the Irish historical narrative, presenting instead a more nationalist reading of Irish history. This proved particularly controversial amongst academic historians, and in 1911 she penned *Irish Nationality;* a more accessible version of Irish history that she intended to be widely circulated amongst ordinary men and women. Her sole contribution to the writing of women's history came in 1897 with *Woman's Place in the World of Letters,* in which she observed; *"In public life we mainly know women as moral reformers, not as political thinkers or zealots for constitutional freedom and development."*

Well known in London's intellectual circles, Alice Stopford Green frequently hosted gatherings at her home in Kensington Square. These were attended by prominent members of the city's literary and cultural scene, including her friends Beatrice Webb, Mary Kingsley and Roger Casement. A growing interest in international political events led her to found the African Society, and in 1901 she travelled to Africa to observe for herself the conditions of prisoners in the Boer War conflict. Her experience there led to her becoming increasingly vociferous in her opposition to British colonialism, and also prompted her to re-evaluate the nature of the constitutional relationship between Britain and her native land.

Educated at home, her father was Rector of Kells and Archdeacon of Meath. In her younger years Alice enjoyed access to her father's substantial library, and was self-taught in subjects including Greek and German. After her father's death she moved to England with her mother and sister, where she met Oxford historian John Richard Green. The couple married in 1877 and set up home in London where Alice assisted her new husband with his research.

Alice Stopford Green died in 1929 at the age of eighty-two, and in the by-election that followed later that year, her seat in the Seanad was won by her friend Kathleen Browne.

"We have shared our country's sorrows, and we expect her joys."

Following her unexpected election to Seanad Eireann in 1922, Alice Stopford Green was inspired to gift a vellum scroll on which the members of the First Seanad were invited to sign their names. Her intention was that this document would be placed on a table at the opening of every meeting of the Seanad to serve as *"a perpetual memorial to the foundation of this body, and a witness in later times of its increasing service to the country"*. The casket was accompanied by an address, which was read into the record by Senator Douglas as Senator Stopford Green was too ill to attend that session. Following the dissolution of the Seanad in 1936 the casket was entrusted to the Royal Irish Academy for safekeeping.

Senator's Gift to the Seanad 26 November 1924

Communication from Senator Mrs. Stopford Green offering a casket for the acceptance of the Seanad.

I ask leave to send a few words as to the casket which I offer to the Seanad.

Senators will agree that we should place no emblem before us in this Assembly that is not of Ireland, in spirit and in workmanship, carrying in it the faith both of the Old Irish world and of the New. I have insisted, therefore, that the form of the casket should go back in direct descent to the "shrines" designed by the Irish over a thousand years ago. The artist has magnificently proved the power of that spiritual inheritance which has been bequeathed to us from an Old Ireland; and has shown that a really living art has no need to copy in slavish routine, and can to-day be as free and original and distinguished as in the times of ancient renown, supposed to have been lost.

Thus the shrine in its intense vitality carries to us its own message. That if we want to revive here an Irish nation we must dig our roots deep into its soil, and be nourished by that ancient earth. In Old Ireland, a land of many peoples, it was not privileges of race that united Irishmen in one country and under one law. It was a common loyalty to the land that bore them. "*This then is my foster-mother, the island in which ye are, even Ireland. Moreover it is the mast and the produce, the flower and the food of this island that have sustained me from the Deluge until to-day.*" This feeling was the refrain of Irish nationality, the loyalty of a people made one by their sonship to the land that bore them, an early and passionate conception of nationality. A sudden and brief outburst by an Irish poet of the old time has no parallel in European mediaeval history—"*The counsels of God concerning virgin Eriú are greater than can be told.*"

From the beginning, Ireland has been rich in her hospitality to men of good-will coming within her borders. And at all times there have been incomers who have honourably responded to that generosity, and have become faithful members of her people. She has had her reward among the strangers who under her wide skies have felt the wonder of the land, and the quality of its people, and have entered into her commonwealth.

Through the long record of wars and assaults, in every generation in turn, men who came as warriors, even the roughest of them, remained as men of Ireland. They took their share in defence of their new home, and endured, if need were, in evil times outrage, ruin and death in the cause of Irish freedom and independence. No real history of Ireland has yet been written. When the true story is finally worked out—one not wholly occupied with the many and insatiable plunderers—it will give us a noble and reconciling vision of Irish nationality. Silence and neglect will no longer hide the fame of honourable men. We shall learn the ties which did in fact ever bind the dwellers in Ireland together. Whether we are of an ancient Irish descent, or of later Irish birth, we are united in one people, and we are bound by one lofty obligation to complete the building of our common nation. We have lived under the breadth of her skies, we have been fed by the fatness of her fields, and nourished by the civilisation of her dead. Our people lie in her earth, and we ourselves must in that earth await our doom. We have shared our country's sorrows, and we expect her joys. "*The mother that has nursed us is she, and when you have looked on her she is not unlovely.*" To Ireland we have given our faith. In Ireland is our hope.

PROUD TO SERVE: The Voices of the Women of Cumann na nGaedheal and Fine Gael 1922-1992

Margaret Collins-O'Driscoll (1920s)
Image courtesy RTÉ Archives

1922–1933 Debating The Exercise of Citizenship For Women

> "When I was elected to the Dáil I was not elected on the question of sex. I gave a pledge to my constituents that I would do my best to serve them and the State."

1923 TD
Margaret Collins-O'Driscoll

Teachta Dála for Dublin North 1923–1933

First female TD elected for Cumann na nGaedheal

Second woman to serve as Vice-President of Cumann na nGaedheal

The only female member of the 6th Dáil

Margaret Collins-O'Driscoll was first elected to represent the constituency of Dublin North in August 1923, in the process becoming the first female TD elected for Cumann na nGaedheal. Margaret got involved in politics after the assassination of her youngest brother Michael Collins, and was elected to the Dáil on her first attempt. Three years after her election, she became the second woman to serve as Vice-President of Cumann na nGaedheal, following the resignation of Jennie Wyse Power. Having successfully retained her seat at the elections of June and September 1927, Margaret was the only female member of the 6th Dáil, which sat during the years 1927 to 1932.

Regarded as an authority on educational questions, the TD for Dublin North frequently referenced her previous work and life experience, and her many contributions to Dáil debates provide an interesting insight into her assertiveness, her no-nonsense approach and her insistence on accuracy in all things. Her speeches also reflect some broader perceptions about the role of women in society at the time. During one debate in 1925 she observed, *"In the days of my youth it was regarded as a qualification for matrimony that a woman should be able to make her husband's shirts"*, while she later expressed her pleasure in voting for the 1928 Censorship of Publications Bill, which banned indecent literature and publications that referred to birth control; *"No vote I have ever given here, or will ever give, will be given with more satisfaction than the vote I will register in favour of this bill."*

Despite a personal belief in equality between the sexes, her parliamentary career was characterised by an unwavering adherence to the party line, which mirrored the overwhelmingly conservative attitude to social issues that prevailed at that time. By the time of the 1933 election she held the record amongst private members for attendance in the division lobbies in support of Government measures. In keeping with this, and despite heavy lobbying by many women requesting that she oppose it on their behalf, she

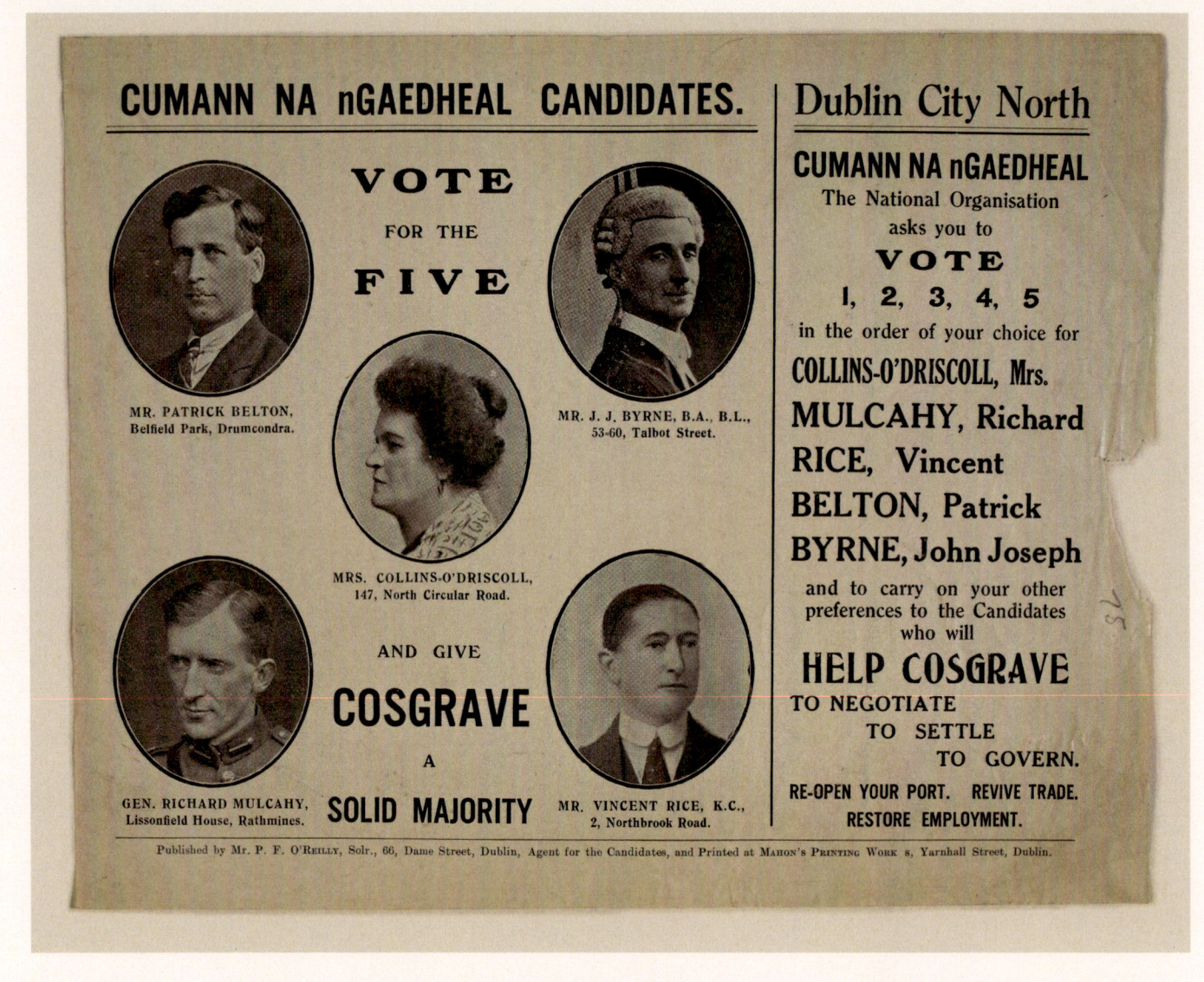

PROUD TO SERVE: The Voices of the Women of Cumann na nGaedheal and Fine Gael 1922-1992

voted with the Government in favour of the 1924 and 1927 Juries Acts, both of which introduced specific provisions pertaining to women serving on juries.

On another occasion, while speaking on the Civil Service Amendment Act, she commented;

"When I was elected to the Dáil I was not elected on the question of sex. I gave a pledge to my constituents that I would do my best to serve them and the State… All I can say to those people who canvassed me to vote against this Bill is that women, when the next election will come on, will have an opportunity to return women on the Government ticket to this Dáil who will have the power to amend this bill if it is passed… I am by no means in love with it and I ask the Minister and the Government to limit the number of appointments as far as possible for which women would be ineligible under this Bill." (Dáil debate on the Civil Service Regulation (Amendment) Bill 1925 Second Stage)

Margaret Collins-O'Driscoll Election Poster 1933, Courtesy of the National Library of Ireland

Not only did Margaret lobby for less restrictions on the number of appointments open to women, she also used this as an opportunity to call on women to elect women, who could then assert their power.

Margaret Collins-O'Driscoll lost her seat at the 1933 election and retired from politics following a parliamentary career spanning ten years.

Born in Co. Cork in 1878, she trained as a national school teacher, and was the principal of Lisvaird Girls' National School close to Clonakilty for many years. The eldest sister of Michael Collins, she married Patrick O'Driscoll, the owner of the West Cork People and they raised a large family of fourteen children, nine girls and five boys. In 1921 the family moved to the North Circular Road in Dublin so that their daughters could receive their third level education there, while Margaret continued her teaching career in Dublin. A grand-aunt to Mary Banotti and Nora Owen, Margaret Collins-O'Driscoll died in Dublin on 17th June, 1945.

The following is an excerpt from a speech given by Margaret Collins-O'Driscoll in 1928, on the subject of vaccinations. She brings her experience as a "family woman" and as a female deputy to bear on the debate, at a time when she was the only female member of the Dáil.

20 April 1928

Private Deputies' Business – Vaccination (Amendment) Bill, 1928 – Second Stage Resumed

I found it very hard to observe the rules of order while my colleague, Deputy J.J. Byrne, was speaking. At almost every sentence I felt inclined to interrupt and contradict him. Speaking on this matter from the point of view of the ordinary lay woman, I say if this conscience clause is passed it will give two classes of mothers in this country a very good excuse for not getting their children vaccinated—(1) those who are too foolishly fond of their children and say they do not want them vaccinated, that vaccination would hurt them; and (2) careless mothers who allow their children to remain unvaccinated. These classes will be conscientious objectors if there is any loophole through which they can avoid the law. I think the House would be criminally guilty if they allowed this conscience clause to pass, thus leaving the young children of the present day, as well as the unborn children of the future, open to such a terrible disease as small-pox. Those of us whose memories go back to the eighties can recall the number of pretty, prepossessing people, as Deputy Wolfe described them, who were hopelessly disfigured by this dire and fell disease. I can remember, in the County Cork, seeing men go around who were afflicted with blindness from the effects of small-pox. I am not concerned with what has happened in Brazil, or with the opinions of Sir Edward Chadwick. What I am concerned with is Ireland, and with what is occurring in our own country, and the fact is that this country has been immune from small-pox since the vaccination laws had to be rigidly adhered to. I am far more concerned with the opinions of Deputy Sir James

Craig than with the opinions of Sir Edward Chadwick. Deputies should realise that there is a terrible responsibility placed upon them before they vote for the conscience clause.

Deputy J.J. Byrne spoke as a family man. I speak as a family woman, and I may mention here that my family runs into two figures. Every one of my children has been vaccinated. The process gave them no pain. I was there myself when the children were vaccinated. They did not even cry during the process. After the vaccination they were ill for a couple of days. But what are the trifling effects that a child may suffer after vaccination compared with the terrible effects that children may suffer from this dire malady of small-pox? I have read some of the objections that in the early days were put up against vaccination. Deputy Byrne's theories seem as ridiculous as many of the objections that were put up when Dr Jenner first discovered the effects of vaccination. It was prophesied that vaccination would brutalise the children; it was averred that the vaccinated children became ox-faced; that abscesses broke out to indicate the spread of horns, and that the countenance of the person affected became gradually transmuted into the visage of a cow, and the voice into the bellowing of bulls. There seems to be about just as much sense and logic in some of the arguments which the anti-vaccinationists have put up in this House as there were in the objections I have just mentioned.

I appeal to Deputies to think of their responsibilities to the children of this country and to oppose this measure of Deputy Everett's. Like Deputy Sir James Craig, I also regard Deputy Everett as a pleasant comrade in this House, and I am sorry to have to oppose him, but my responsibilities are far too great, and I therefore appeal to the House to reject this measure.

"I speak as a family woman, and I may mention here that my family runs into two figures."

DÁIL ELECTIONS, 1933.

DUBLIN CITY NORTH.

Polling Tuesday, 24th January, 1933,
9 a.m. to 9 p.m.

The Cumann na nGaedheal

Candidates are shown in **Heavy Type** below. Vote **1, 2, 3, 4, 5,** for them in the order of your choice.

Mark this Card and bring it with you. It will help you to mark your Voting Paper.

No.	Name
	BELTON, P.
	BREATHNACH, C.
	BYRNE, A.
	BYRNE, J. J.
	COLLINS-O'DRISCOLL, Mrs.
	COONEY, E.
	LARKIN, J.
	MULCAHY, R.
	O'KELLY, S. T.
	O'SULLIVAN, M.
	RICE, V.
	STAFFORD, M.
	TRAYNOR, O.

Give No. 6 or other preferences to the other Candidates opposed to the present Government.

Published by Patrick F. O'Reilly, Solicitor, 66 Dame Street, Dublin, Election Agent for the Candidates and Printed by Browne & Nolan, Ltd., 41 & 42 Nassau Street, Dublin.

Election ephemera, 1933
Courtesy of the National Library of Ireland

PROUD TO SERVE: The Voices of the Women of Cumann na nGaedheal and Fine Gael 1922-1992

Kathleen Browne
Photograph used with the kind permission of Des Walsh

> "I, personally, know of many cases where … if the woman were prevented from doing certain work, it would mean great hardship and, possibly, the starvation of the family."

1929 SENATOR
Kathleen A. Browne

Senator 1929-1936
Executive Committee Member Cumann na Saoirse
Member of Cumann na mBan
Member of The Irish Countrywomen's Association

Kathleen Browne's political interest can be traced as far back as the early 1880s when, at the age of five, she became a member of the local Ladies' Land League in Kilmore. This early interest in rural affairs and farmer's rights proved enduring and in later years, in addition to her day-to-day work as *"a practical farmer"*, she became an expert in dairy management, a subject on which she lectured for several years with the Department of Agriculture. Her myriad interests encompassed subjects beyond the world of politics and farming, and included areas such as archaeology, the Irish language and making the history of her native Wexford more widely accessible. She was also an expert with specialist knowledge of the local Wexford dialect of Yola.

A romantic nationalist, Kathleen's intense interest in the issues of the day resulted in her enthusiastic membership of a number of organisations including the Gaelic League, Sinn Féin, the Irish Volunteers and Cumann na mBan. An accomplished artist and writer in her own right, she was drawn to the cultural revival movement, and organised a number of successful Feis Charman in Wexford. In the 1920s and 30s she joined Cumann na nGaedheal, the Blueshirts (the Army Comrades' Association and the National Guard) and Fine Gael. She was also a member of the Irish Countrywomen's Association.

Having joined Sinn Féin in 1912, Kathleen became an active member of the Party's Ard Comhairle in Wexford, and quickly developed a reputation as an impassioned public speaker. Her public pronouncements brought her to the attention of the Royal Irish Constabulary who noted that; *"Few women in this country achieved such fame as Miss Browne … and her outspoken and uncompromising addresses from public platforms reflected the strength and sincerity of her convictions."* She joined the Irish Volunteers in 1914, later taking an active part in the 1916 Rising in Wexford where her activities included raising the tricolour above the family home and helping to take the Athenaeum in Enniscorthy. These actions resulted in her imprisonment in Waterford Jail, Richmond Barracks, Kilmainham Gaol and Mountjoy Gaol. Kathleen's incarceration in Kilmainham Gaol coincided with the executions of the leaders of 1916, and she later confided to her friend Alice Stopford Green, *"I was glad to be in prison and to have a slight share in the sufferings of our latest martyrs."* In 1918 she worked with Alice Furlong to organise Lá na mBan (Women's Day), was active in the anti-conscription campaign and also canvassed for Jim Ryan who was elected as a Sinn Féin member of Wexford South County Constituency that year.

Kathleen took the pro-Treaty side during the Civil War, and when Cumann na mBan divided along pro and anti-Treaty lines, she broke with her former comrades to join the newly established pro-Treaty women's organisation Cumann na Saoirse. The Civil War and its aftermath proved an especially bitter experience for her. Her farming produce was boycotted as a result of the politics she espoused, and in March 1924 she received the sum of £200 from the Dáil Special Fund to compensate her for the losses she had endured. The divisiveness and bitterness of those years proved longstanding, and many of her close personal associations and friendships were irreparably damaged.

In 1922 Kathleen Browne was the main Cumann na nGaedheal party organiser in her native Wexford. She was appointed a Peace Commissioner in 1925 and unsuccessfully contested the Senate Election of that year. On 20th June, 1929 she was elected to the First Seanad as a Cumann na nGaedheal member at the by-election caused by the death of her friend Alice Stopford Green. Re-elected in 1931 and again in 1934, she was an active member of the National Guard. She caused considerable disquiet by wearing her blue blouse in Seanad Eireann, an act which paved the way for the introduction of the Wearing of Uniforms Restrictions Bill of 1934.

Despite being socially conservative and a staunch Catholic, Kathleen's contributions to debates in Seanad Éireann show that she consistently opposed legislation limiting the role of women in society. She also supported farmers' rights and as a member of the Irish Countrywomen's Association she was very aware of the gender inequalities in Irish rural society at that time, a topic she referred to in many debates on agriculture. Her knowledge and experience did not make her immune from pejorative comments. In response to a query she raised during a debate on the Public Services (Temporary Economies) Bill on 16th August, 1933, Fianna Fáil Senator Michael Comyn retorted disparagingly, *"Senator Miss Browne is very fond of the Army. Girls are always fond of military men."*

Kathleen Browne joined Fine Gael in 1933, retiring from public life when the Free State Seanad was abolished on 29th May, 1936. Following her days in the Seanad she remained active in political circles, campaigning on a number of issues. In addition to her work as a farmer, she also continued to help her sister Maisie raise the children of another sister who had died in 1927. Kathleen died of cardiac failure on 9th October, 1943. She was sixty-five years of age.

Born in Bridgetown, Co. Wexford in 1876, her father Michael was involved in the local land agitation movement prior to becoming a member of Wexford's first County Council in 1899. In September 2018 Bridgetown Historical

> *"I was glad to be in prison and to have a slight share in the sufferings of our latest martyrs."*

Society hosted the inaugural Kathleen Browne Arts and Literary Festival, and a plaque was unveiled at the house where she was born by one of her relatives, the psychiatrist Dr Ivor Browne.

The following two excerpts come from speeches made by Kathleen Browne in the Seanad in 1930 and 1935 respectively and show some of the attitudes then prevalent towards women.

19 March 1930

Illegitimate Children (Affiliation Orders) Bill, 1929

I am afraid that the conditions which Senator Moore spoke of might have applied thirty or forty years ago; they certainly do not apply now. However, I agree from my experience in an absolutely rural district, that the vast majority of these unfortunate girls are comparatively innocent of the crime they commit. They are trapped into this unfortunate state, and from the cases that have come under my notice, I am absolutely certain that not one in a thousand would go into a public court, though they might go into a court where the evidence would be heard in camera. Of course, there are hardened sinners who certainly might try to blackmail a man. That might apply in a city, but not in the country, except in very few cases. The vast majority of these girls are young and comparatively innocent, and they certainly would not go into a public court. I think they would die rather than face a public court, where they would be held up to the contempt of all the loafers and idlers who would go to the court to gloat over their misery. I support the provision for the hearing of cases in camera.

12 December 1935

Conditions of Employment Bill, 1935 — Committee Stage

I wish to agree with the amendment, not because I am as familiar with the matter as the proposers of the amendment are, but because I have made all the inquiries and investigations that I could make to enlighten me on this matter and, as a result of these inquiries, have come to the conclusion that this section should not be in the Bill and that it would be much better if it were deleted. As Senator Brown said, the employment of women is a very difficult matter indeed to deal with, and I hope that his suggestion with regard to special legislation will be carefully considered, because it is an urgent matter. None of us, I think, wants to see the condition, which was described by certain members of the Labour Party, where the man stays at home and the woman goes out to earn the bread for the family; but I, personally, know of many cases where that condition was an absolute necessity and where, if the woman were prevented from doing certain work, it would mean great hardship and, possibly, the starvation of the family.

PROUD TO SERVE: The Voices of the Women of Cumann na nGaedheal and Fine Gael 1922-1992

top left Mary Reynolds and her mother Mary Smith at their family home Drumcoura Lake, circa 1920s
top right Reynolds Family, circa 1960
left Reynolds Family, 1931
Courtesy of Noeleen Smith and the Reynolds Family

> "I have laboured unselfishly in furthering the individual and collective interests of my constituents, which efforts have met with a large measure of success."

1932 TD
Mary Reynolds

Teachta Dála for Leitrim-Sligo 1932–1933; 1937–1961

First female Cumann na nGaedheal TD for Leitrim-Sligo

Successful in all but one of the election campaigns she contested throughout her time in politics

Such was the bitterness engendered by the Irish Civil War that violence was still a regular feature of political involvement at the time. The election of Mary Reynolds to Dáil Eireann took place in shocking and dramatic circumstances. On the eve of the 1932 general election, word reached her that her husband Paddy, who had been a Cumann na nGaedheal TD, had been fatally shot while out canvassing. As the rest of the country went to the polls, the general election was postponed in the constituency for two weeks. Having just buried her husband, the bereaved Mary Reynolds was nominated to contest the election. She ran a successful election campaign and was the first female TD for the Leitrim-Sligo Constituency.

Following her election, she joined fellow Cumann na nGaedheal TD Margaret Collins-O'Driscoll in the chamber of Dáil Eireann in 1932. She narrowly lost her seat at the general election of 1933, but was returned to the Dáil to represent the newly named constituency of Sligo-Leitrim in 1937, successfully contesting every subsequent election until her retirement in 1961.

In her first year as a deputy, Mary Reynolds entrusted the care of her seven children, then aged between fifteen and four, to her mother who lived with the family, following which Mrs Reynolds, as she was known by everyone, quickly set to work. A personable, unassuming woman, she proved tireless in her efforts on behalf of her constituents. Her Dáil contributions were mainly confined to parliamentary questions and as an obituary notice observed; *"she did not make very many speeches, but her dealings with ministers and those in authority were characterised by a personal approach."* She always went directly to the doors of those concerned to make representations on behalf of her constituents. She frequently visited Leitrim patients in Dublin hospitals, later relaying details of their progress to family members who were unable to travel to see them in Dublin.

Generally regarded as *"good for a lift"*, the lorry belonging to the family business was often availed of by constituents travelling to Dublin, and also on occasion by Mrs Reynolds herself, who did not drive. A daily mass goer, her strong faith sustained her through difficult times, particularly after the deaths of two of her children, one of whom died in an accident in America. Successful in nine election campaigns, news of her election victories were communicated locally using a pre-arranged system, whereby one person went into a field and let a cheer, which was then carried by another person standing on a hill nearby who heard the shout and passed it on. In this way word of her election spread throughout the community, while bonfires were also lit in celebration.

Born in Drumcoura, Co. Leitrim on 5th October, 1889, Mary Reynolds (neé Smith) was educated at Drumreilly National School, and spent her last year at the Convent School in Ballinamore. On completion of her schooling she emigrated to New York. It was there, in 1915, that she married Leitrim man Paddy Reynolds and the couple had two children before returning home to Ireland in 1919. They purchased a farm and later opened a grocery bar and light hardware store on the main street in Ballinamore. Patrick J. Reynolds, her son, won the seat in the election following her retirement, while her grandson Gerry Reynolds was also a Senator and later a TD for the Sligo - Leitrim Constituency. By all accounts Mary Reynolds was a widely respected figure, both locally and in Leinster House. She died on 24th August, 1974.

"If elected, I shall be a representative of my constituents as a whole and not of any section thereof."

The following is the text of an election address published by Mary Reynolds in 1954, which gives some insight into her interests and her focus on the concerns of her constituents.

Ballinamore, Co. Leitrim, 5th May, 1954
ELECTION ADDRESS FROM MRS. MARY REYNOLDS

A Chairde,

The disapproval of Fianna Fáil policy expressed by the electors of Wicklow, Limerick, Dublin, Louth, Cork County and City has clearly indicated that Fianna Fáil no longer has the confidence of the people of the country and, consequently, a General Election has been declared.

I have again been unanimously selected to contest the Sligo-Leitrim Constituency in the interests of Fine Gael. My unanimous selection and the fact that I was placed at the head of the poll at the last election show that my services in the past have been appreciated. I sincerely wish to thank all those voters who, by giving me their No.1 and other preferences, placed me at the head of the poll. To those who worked so unselfishly to secure my return at the last and other elections I desire to express my deepest gratitude.

Hereunder are a few reasons why you should support the Fine Gael and the other inter-party candidates at the forthcoming election:-

1) A well-ordered Agricultural Policy means prosperity for the farmer and consequently, prosperity for the village, prosperity for the town, prosperity for the nation.

2) Fine Gael proposes to establish an Institute of Veterinary and Agricultural Science and bring the latest methods and most scientific knowledge to the farmer's door.

3) Fine Gael will again fully implement the Land Rehabilitation Scheme – a scheme which apparently has received the go-slow order under the Fianna Fáil regime.

4) To reduce the cost of production, the Inter-Party Government will remove all taxes on fertilizers and other raw materials of agriculture. This is the only country in which the imported materials for agriculture are taxed.

The Fianna Fáil administration has increased taxation - direct and indirect - and thus forced up the cost of living to a record high level. Just compare your weekly shopping bill for essential goods today with your weekly shopping bill under the Inter-Party Government. This crippling taxation has brought business to a stand-still in our towns and villages, reduced employment and brought emigration to a record high figure, while millions of pounds are set aside for unnecessary and unproductive schemes, such as the Bray Road and Dublin Castle. The four million pounds to be spent on Dublin Castle would go a long way towards reconstructing every farmer's house in need of reconstruction. The six hundred thousand pounds to be spent on the Bray Road would do much with the bye-roads and laneways of Ireland and give much needed employment to our labourers and small farmers in counties such as Leitrim and Sligo.

The limited space of time at my disposal before election day may not afford me an opportunity of a personal call on all the electors, consequently I am issuing this appeal for your support. During the years it has been my privilege to represent you in Dáil Eireann, I have laboured unselfishly in furthering the individual and collective interests of my constituents, which efforts have met with a large measure of success.

In conclusion, I promise, as on previous occasions, that, if elected, I shall be a representative of my constituents as a whole and not of any section thereof.

Mise, le meas,

MARY REYNOLDS

VOTE THUS:

1. REYNOLDS, MARY 2. FALLON, THOMAS

AND FOR THE OTHER FINE GAEL AND INTER-PARTY CANDIDATES IN THE ORDER OF YOUR CHOICE

Printed at the "OBSERVER" Works, Carrick-on-Shannon, and published by the Candidate.

CUMANN NA nGAEDHEAL MEETING AT CAPPOQUIN.—Mrs. Redmond (marked X) addressing the crowd at a Cumann na nGaedheal meeting in Cappoquin, Co. Waterford. (Doyle, Cappoquin).

Cumann na nGaedheal Meeting at Cappoquin
Courtesy of the National Library of Ireland

> "It will be a bad day for Ireland when the housewives are without adequate technical knowledge of the responsibilities they assume."

1933 TD
Bridget Mary Redmond

Teachta Dála for Waterford 1933–1952

First female Fine Gael TD for Waterford

Exemplary Dáil attendance record

Bridget Mary Redmond was the first female Fine Gael TD for Waterford, a constituency she represented for nineteen years. Her diligence in relation to constituency matters ensured that she successfully retained her seat at seven general elections. Bridget's Dáil attendance record was exemplary and she submitted parliamentary questions relating to a variety of constituency matters on a regular basis. During the debate on the draft 1937 Constitution, she proposed an amendment to Article 9, that no citizen shall be placed by law under any such disability or incapacity by reason of sex, class or religion. It was unsuccessful.

Born in Kildare in 1905, she was the eldest daughter of John and Bridget Mallick, where her father was a business man who owned a number of successful steeplechasers. The family were well known in Irish horse racing circles and in her early years particularly, Bridget was herself a keen and enthusiastic horsewoman. She completed her education at the Ursuline Convent in Waterford, and at the age of twenty-five married Waterford TD and barrister Capt. William (Willie) Redmond, the only son of Irish Parliamentary Party leader John Redmond MP.

Following Willie's death at the age of forty-five, just two years into their marriage, his young widow successfully contested the general election for Cumann na nGaedheal. Bridget's election to represent the people of Waterford in 1933 was viewed as an extension of the parliamentary connection between the Redmond family and Irish politics stretching back to 1891.

Her contributions to Dáil debates demonstrate her interest in a spectrum of issues including tourism, fisheries, agriculture, education and finance. During a debate on the Racing Board and Racecourses Bill of 1945 she supported an amendment giving bookmakers the right to appeal decisions of the Racing Board, arguing that bookmaking; *"is as honourable a business as any other,*

above Mrs Redmond
Courtesy of the National Library of Ireland

and there are as decent men connected with it as are to be found in any other sphere." In her contribution to the committee on Finance Bill on Industry and Commerce in 1948, she suggested that it might be a help if;

"Instead of having men inspecting the various hotels, lady inspectors were appointed. They would be able to get down to rock-bottom and to ensure that the visitors would have the benefit of the things that count most to them."

In the area of education, Bridget frequently extolled the benefits of the Technical School system and the value to both girls and boys of the practical skills being imparted there. She argued that all of the country's school-goers would benefit from a period spent being educated in such technical institutes, something she felt was particularly important given the school leaving age, which was then fourteen. She believed it was vital to *"encourage the children to have other interests in addition to book learning"* observing that; *"We should try to prepare the children of the present day at school for what they have to do to earn their living in order to keep themselves and their families later on."*

Bridget Redmond died on 3rd May, 1952 and news of her death from pulmonary tuberculosis at the age of forty-seven came as a shock to many. Her obituary in the *Leinster Leader* of 10th May, 1952 concluded that; *"The extent of her good work in Waterford and Kildare, will perhaps never be fully measured, but there are many in both counties who can thank the good offices of the late Mrs. Redmond for something which had helped to ease the burden of life."*

Bridget Redmond's Dáil contributions often centred on education, particularly her belief that both boys and girls should avail of the training being imparted at technical colleges before they completed their education, as evidenced in the following excerpt from 1947.

20 May 1947

Vote 45 — Office of the Minister for Education (Resumed)

Perhaps the Minister in his own wise judgment could conceive some plan whereby our young boys could receive more extensive instruction in agriculture which, as we are often told, is the main industry of the country. We rely on agriculture for our principal exports and in return we rely on it to provide the money to pay for our imports. If the Minister does not consider it possible to raise the school-leaving age, perhaps he might consider giving some further grants to schools to enable them to give agricultural instruction to boys in the 14 years' category. So far as girls in the country are concerned, in many cases they have not sufficient wisdom to attend technical schools on their own initiative or, perhaps, their parents do not realise sufficiently the importance of sending them to such schools.

In my opinion, these schools are very much neglected in the country. Only last week I read in a daily newspaper, I think it was the Independent, of some

> *"We should try to prepare the children of the present day at school for what they have to do to earn their living in order to keep themselves and their families later on."*

resolution, proposing to close down one or two technical schools in a particular county owing to insufficient attendance. I think that is a great mistake having regard to the amount of money that has been expended by the Department of Education on these schools. Now that these schools are in existence, I think that an effort should be made to make girls appreciate the subjects taught in these schools which would be very useful to them in after life. Whether they intend to take up a profession or other employment, or whether they intend to stay at home, they will, probably, get married eventually, and be the wives in the future Ireland. It will be a bad day for Ireland when the housewives are without adequate technical knowledge of the responsibilities they assume. Long ago, we were proud of our domestic accomplishments. Now, I am afraid that girls in the country are not sufficiently keen on acquiring ordinary, technical school knowledge on these matters. I ask the Minister to enlist the good offices of the teachers in this connection. We are grateful to the teachers for the example of self-denial they show in carrying out their heavy task throughout the year. Could the Minister not arrange to have lectures delivered to the children, impressing the necessity upon them, when they finish their ordinary school career at the age of 14, of taking advantage of the technical schools? The knowledge they would acquire would be of great value to them in after life, even if they did not appreciate it at the time.

I ask the Minister to arrange for a series of lectures to children due to leave school in June or July each year, by persons authorised by the Department, urging them to attend the technical schools. Those who went before them would long ago have been only too pleased to take advantage of such facilities. They would not regard it as a penalty to be required to attend but they would regard it as something in the nature of an achievement and would have been proud to educate themselves for their future lives. The Minister should institute some system such as this. At present, we have these wonderful schools, with excellent teachers, but they are not being availed of as they should.

1957-1979
Shaping The Power of Politics For Women

PROUD TO SERVE: The Voices of the Women of Cumann na nGaedheal and Fine Gael 1922-1992

> *"Women politicians have to work 25 per cent harder to get the same number of votes"*

1957 TD
Brigid Hogan-O'Higgins

Teachta Dála for Galway South 1957–1961

Teachta Dála for Galway East 1961–1969

Teachta Dála for Clare-Galway South 1969–1977

First woman to represent Galway in Dáil Éireann

Fine Gael Spokesman for Posts and Telegraphs 1969-1972

Acting Chairman for a number of debates in the Dáil between 1973 and 1977

The first woman to represent Galway in Dáil Éireann, Brigid Hogan was elected, at almost twenty-four years of age, as a TD for the then Galway South Constituency in 1957. Brigid spent the majority of her twenty years as a TD in opposition, with the exception of one four-year period between 1973 and 1977 when Fine Gael were in government.

She successfully retained her seat at four subsequent elections, as boundary changes saw the constituency become Galway East in 1961 and 1965, and then Clare-Galway South in 1969 and 1973. In addition to raising issues affecting the people of Galway at national level, her Dáil contributions demonstrate her keen interest in education, health, communications and finance. Brigid was the Party spokesman for Posts and Telegraphs from 1969 to 1972, and was later Acting Chairman for a number of debates in the Dáil during the four-year period when Fine Gael were in government between 1973 and 1977.

Born in Co. Galway in March 1932, her father Patrick Hogan TD was Minister for Agriculture in the first Cumann na nGaedheal Government. He served as TD for Galway from 1921 until his death in a car accident in 1936, when Brigid was just four years of age.

When she married fellow TD Michael O'Higgins a year after first being elected, they became the first married couple to sit in the Dáil. Following her defeat at the 1977 election Brigid Hogan-O'Higgins retired from politics, after which, in addition to rearing a family of nine and managing the family farm, she became actively involved in the local branch of St Vincent de Paul.

Sunday Independent, 1975
Courtesy of Irish Newspaper Archive

The following excerpts are taken from a speech made by Brigid Hogan-O'Higgins in 1976, during her final term in the Dáil. Her contribution contains a number of observations about the attitudes encountered by working women in Ireland at the time, and is particularly enlightening in relation to women and politics.

1 December 1976
Anti-Discrimination (Employment) Bill, 1975, Second Stage

In welcoming this Bill Deputy Hogan-O'Higgins emphasised the following:

Women complain now that they have little say in politics but the situation has come about by reason of their reluctance to get in and fight their way up. Regardless of what anyone on either side of the House may say, I know that men resent women in politics. I recall an incident in 1965 when a senior Member of this House asked me if I intended re-contesting the general election to be held in that year. When I told him it was my intention to go forward again, he asked me if I did not consider Leinster House an unsuitable place for a lady. In reply I told him that I had never had any ambition to be a lady but that I always had held a wish to remain in politics. The idea that ladies do not work is a nonsensical hangover from the Victorian era.

In regard to equal opportunity—and this is what I consider to be the most important aspect of this whole subject —girls must accept that if they are receiving equal pay they must be prepared to undertake equal work. I know of a hospital in which equal pay was granted, not to the nursing staff but to other staff, some time ago but where some of the women workers decided that they would not undertake to work at night although they wished to be able to continue to receive equal pay.

I trust that employers will be able to rid themselves of the notion that once a woman marries she will be a liability in some way to the firm because of working time that may be lost as a result of pregnancies. That attitude tends to discriminate against women being employed. Employers should regard all candidates as potential employees rather than to segregate them on a sex basis. Women who find it necessary because of pregnancies to leave work for a short while should be entitled to return to their jobs if they so wish. It is fashionable at the moment to criticise married women for going out to work but even if all the married women who are employed outside their homes were to relinquish their employment, the impact on the employment situation would be very small in terms of the numbers of jobs that would become available for other people.

Another factor in this is that very often the jobs undertaken by married women would not be undertaken by single people. In regard to this whole question we must consider our entire system of education. It is my contention that married women are as much entitled to work as is anybody else. Recently I attended a meeting—it was not political—at which there was expressed much criticism of married women who go to work. Afterwards I spoke to one of the men who

Connacht Tribune, 1957
Courtesy of Irish Newspaper Archive

had been most vociferous on the subject and, referring to the fact that he had quite a number of daughters, I asked whether he would not wish them to go to work after they had been through university. This man's situation is not such as to warrant his children being eligible for free education at third level. I asked him whether, if any of his girls should marry in her final year at the university, it would be his idea that she should not follow a career. He became quite indignant and said that he would expect them to follow careers after so much money had been spent on them.

It is a feature of a period of economic recession that where there are men and women employed in the lower paid jobs, the tendency is to employ men rather than women as vacancies occur. This is particularly noticeable in regard to such categories of workers as waitresses, shop assistants and so on. This is the case also in other countries. A person who holds a senior position in the civil service in Italy told me that this is the case in that country. This sort of discrimination should not be practised. In the lower paid jobs women are to blame in regard to promotion in so far as they are reluctant to assume posts of responsibility.

Recently in my constituency I attended the official opening of a big extension to a factory. On the occasion the management paid much tribute to those girls who had been with the firm from the time of its inception and who were responsible for much of the success of the venture. Afterwards I spoke to the manager who was an American and asked him how many of those girls now held senior jobs with the company. He replied that although the girls had been offered more responsible positions, they had refused to accept them. This attitude indicates a lack of education, a lack of confidence. It is a hangover from the Victorian era that girls are taught to regard themselves as not as adequate, perhaps, as men in employment.

More and more married women are working and they are perfectly entitled to work for whatever reasons, but they should provide, where they can afford it, an adequate child-minding service for themselves. Many parents—both working in good jobs, as Deputy Enright said—do not provide this and they could do so out of their own resources. I realise that women working because of necessity and because money is very scarce are not able to pay somebody to look after the children and that the State has a certain duty to provide some type of day centre or crèches. The larger factories should also provide these facilities. Many of the large industries are making enormous profits and the small cost of providing a day centre or crèche would be well worth while. They would gain happier employees and in the long run this would benefit the industry.

Deputy Hogan-O'Higgins also referred to the prevention of gender discrimination in social welfare.

It is incredible that in this day and age there should be discrimination between men and women in the social welfare field. Mark you, I have reservations here. I do not think that school leavers of any age should get unemployment assistance. It tends to keep them on the dole and discourage them from seeking work. The young people all think they should start at the top.

> "It is a hangover from the Victorian era that girls are taught to regard themselves as not as adequate, perhaps, as men in employment."

I think if they did not have social welfare they would take any sort of job and make "*a go*" of it if they were any good. At present they seem to think they must start at the top or they will not take the job. This is a mistake. I think it is wrong to give unemployment assistance to either boys or girls in the first year of their leaving school. It tends to encourage them to idle and this is not what we want in this society.

We have reached a situation where we have a sort of equal pay system but it discriminates between one woman and another, married and single. This will have to be rectified. I sympathise with the Minister because, having made these promises which I really believe the Government meant to carry out, things in the economic field did not turn out as hoped and we are in an economic recession at present. But that does not—nothing does—justify discrimination, and every effort must be made despite the recession to give equal opportunities to men and women.

And, finally an indication of Deputy Hogan-O'Higgins nuanced perspective on "women's libbers".

Discrimination against the female sex for so long has resulted in the vocal element being extremely vocal and they can do themselves a certain amount of harm. In England women now feel that the "*women's libbers*" have done a great deal of harm. Now when they become divorced and have better-paid jobs than their husbands, they have to pay their husbands alimony. Also, in England, a woman's job must be held for her for a year after a pregnancy and this discourages employment of married women. This is why we must have a sense of balance. "Women's libbers" should not go too far and leave women at a disadvantage again so that they would be not only calling the tune but paying for it also.

I have never believed in "women's lib" to any great extent, as I have said over and over again. I do not believe in separate societies; I believe in an integrated society. I believe that men and women complement each other and work very well as a team. Because of the natural bias in society against women, women who get into well-paid jobs work about 25 per cent harder than men to prove their worth because all the time there is this bias against a woman and she must go on proving that she is as valuable to her employer as a man. Deputy Geoghegan-Quinn will probably agree with me in thinking that women politicians have to work 25 per cent harder to get the same number of votes. They start under a handicap and so must be that bit better than the men to be elected. No male Deputy will admit this.

PROUD TO SERVE: The Voices of the Women of Cumann na nGaedheal and Fine Gael 1922-1992

Mrs. Burke is elected with a bigger majority for Fine Gael

"Irish Independent" Reporter

MRS. JOAN BURKE, 36-year-old widow and mother of two children, retained her husband's seat in the Dail for Fine Gael in the Roscommon-south Leitrim by-election yesterday. She was elected with 18,754 votes on the second count, as against 15,673 for the Fianna Fail candidate, Dr. Hugh Gibbons.

[Editorial comment, Page 16]

Mrs. Burke headed the poll with an amazingly high vote of 17,308 first preferences. This was a spectacular success for Fine Gael as it was an increase of 7,334 votes, more than 70 per cent on the party's vote of 9,974 in the 1961 general election.

Fianna Fail also improved their poll considerably, from 10,838 to 15,107 first preferences for Dr. Gibbons. This was a feature of the election — the substantial improvement by the two major parties who, apparently, captured between them the 8,000 to 9,000 floating votes.

Labour did not do as well as was thought originally, but their candidate, Mr. Oliver Macklin, faced some severe obstacles, such as lack of Labour sympathy in the area. He was also, of course, without the powerful election machinery of the other two parties.

LOST DEPOSITS

With only 2,056 first preferences he failed to get the full vote polled by Mr. Jack McQuillan, T.D., now a member of the Labour Party, but who, as a N.P.D. candidate, headed the poll with 5,289 votes in the 1961 election.

Mr. Macklin and the fourth candidate, Mr. Padraig O Ceallaigh (352 votes), the Independent Republican, lost their deposits of £100.

Mrs. Burke had a majority of 1,342 over the quota of 17,412 when she was elected. She received huge support from the electorate of mid-Roscommon, where she lives, and also of west-Roscommon. The voting in south Leitrim, with an electorate of about 9,000, was fairly evenly divided between Mrs. Burke and Dr. Gibbons.

LOUD APPLAUSE

Mrs. Burke's election came on the second count, when she received 1,446 transfers following the elimination of Mr. O Ceallaigh and Mr. Macklin. Dr. Gibbons got 566 votes on the second count.

Loud and prolonged applause from the crowded chamber in Roscommon Courthouse greeted the result when it was announced by the Returning Officer, Mr. P. J. Flynn.

First to congratulate Mrs. Burke were Dr. Gibbons and Mr. Brian Lenihan, Parliamentary Secretary. Her speech of thanks was interrupted several times by applause, especially when she

Continued on Page 17

Mrs. Joan Burke

FIFTH WOMAN DEPUTY

MRS. JOAN BURKE'S election brings representation by women in the Dáil to five. She will partner Mrs. Brigid Hogan O'Higgins on the Fine Gael benches. Across the floor of the House from them will be Mrs. Honor Crowley (Kerry), Mrs. Celia Lynch (Dublin) and Mrs. Sheila Galvin (Cork) of Fianna Fáil.

The successful candidate is 36 and the mother of two children, a girl and a boy. She is a native of Cork and, before her marriage to the late Mr. James Burke, T.D., was a nurse.

There are now two Corkwomen in the Dáil, as Mrs. Galvin won the Cork city by-election caused by the death of her husband. The south Leitrim portion of Mrs. Burke's constituency was formerly represented by a woman Mrs. Brigid Reynolds, T.D.

PARTY POLICY VINDICATED —MR. DILLON

"Irish Independent" Political Correspondent

"APATHY is not a feature of Irish by-elections," Mr. James Dillon, the Fine Gael leader, said from his hospital bed in Dublin last night on being told of the party's win in Roscommon.

He described their victory as a "splendid vindication of Fine Gael policy."

The Taoiseach, Mr. Lemass, said the ground had been well laid for gaining the seat for Fianna Fail in the next General Election, and he regarded as "very encouraging" their increase in first preferences from 31% at the 1961 General Election to 43% in the by-election.

The Labour Leader, Mr. Corish, said the resources used against them had been formidable and thousands of the votes in the total cast would come to Labour in a general election. He interpreted the total vote against the Government as evidence of the public's displeasure with present policies.

NO CHANGE

The result leaves the party position in the Dáil unchanged.— Fianna Fail 71, Fine Gael 47, Labour 18 and others, eight. The new deputy, Mrs. Joan Burke, will not be formally introduced to the Ceann Comhairle until the House resumes after the summer recess. She probably will sign the roll of deputies at Leinster House, however, early next week.

The normal practice is that

Fine Gael policy. I thank all the people of Roscommon and Leitrim and the many others —deputies, senators and Fine Gael workers from constituencies outside Roscommon-Leitrim — who contributed their due share to the victory.

"It is good to see that the voters could be neither bribed

To Page 17

FORGED LETTER

Gardai to make inquiries

GARDA authorities are to be asked to investigate the forged letter received by a farmer in the Boyle area in connection with the Roscommon by-election.

At the count in Roscommon yesterday, the Parliamentary Secretary to the Minister for Lands, Mr. Brian Lenihan, told an Irish Independent reporter that when he gets the letter he will turn it over to the Gardai for a full investigation.

The letter, purporting to be signed by him is in the

£165 FOR DONKEY

MR. P. J. O'MAHONY, of Micorragh, Ballinacarriga, Dunman-

Hopeful aspirants

A few of the hopeful aspirants for the coveted title of "Miss Universe," to be staged at Miami next month. In front are Miss Nigeria (Edma Park) and Miss Turkey (Mlle. Caliskan), while behind (extreme left) are Miss France (Edith Noel) and Miss Spain (Maria Jose Ulla). The picture was taken at Orly airport, Paris, just before the girls set off for America.

BIG REWARD OFFERED IN JEWELS CASE

A £10,000 REWARD was offered yesterday by a London firm for information on the diamonds valued £103,000 stolen on Sunday from a freight terminal at Shannon Airport.

Dangerfield and Co., a firm of loss adjusters, of Lloyd's Avenue, said that the reward would be paid "to the first person giving such information as will lead to the apprehension and conviction of the thief or thieves and to the recovery of the property intact or in proportion."

Files on previous jewel robberies were examined at Interpol HQ in Paris yesterday and in Amsterdam the staff of the jewellers who consigned the diamonds to Ennis Diamond Co., were questioned.

Garda authorities throughout the country and Interpol are looking for a small dark man who speaks with a

TWO THEORIES

There are two theories on which the police are working. The man on getting the diamonds may have boarded a KLM aircraft for New York on Sunday evening or he may be lying low in this country.

It is believed that there might be little difficulty in getting the packet containing the diamonds out of the country as it measured only

5 ft. 7 ins., of sallow complexion, a long face, thin build, possibly a moustache and glasses. He was wearing a dark coat which could be a crombie or garberdine.

1957–1979 Shaping The Power of Politics For Women

> "As a woman in politics you have to be one step ahead of your male colleagues at all times and work that bit harder!"

1964 TD
Joan Burke

Teachta Dála for Roscommon 1964–1969

Teachta Dála for Roscommon-Leitrim 1969–1981

The first woman to represent the people of Roscommon in Dáil Éireann

Topped the poll at each of the five elections she contested

The first woman to represent the people of Roscommon in Dáil Éireann, Joan Burke was selected to contest the Roscommon by-election which took place in July 1964. She succeeded in topping the poll on her first attempt, an enviable feat which she managed to repeat in each of the four elections she subsequently contested. She was again returned to represent the Roscommon Constituency in the general election of 1965, and when boundary changes resulted in the constituency becoming Roscommon-Leitrim in 1969, she held her seat that year, and again at the elections of 1973 and 1977.

Addressing the Annual Dinner of the Irish Widows Association in Athlone on Saturday, 5th April, 1975, Joan remarked that she had *"read recently in Ted Nealon's useful Directory that of the 144 members of the Dáil no less than thirty-one of the male Deputies are sons of previous Deputies"*, while another half dozen were related to former Deputies in other ways. At the time there were just five women in the Dáil, leading Joan to assert that; *"as a woman in politics you have to be one step ahead of your male colleagues at all times and work that bit harder!"*

Throughout her time in politics Joan Burke was vocally opposed to the marriage bar which prohibited married women from working in the public sector. Tax was another area where working women faced discrimination, particularly the Income Tax Act of 1967, which deemed the income of a married woman living with her husband as her husband's income for tax purposes. In 1977 an organisation called the Married Persons Tax Reform Association (MPTRA) began an active campaign for reform in the area. Fianna Fáil's George Colley who was then Minister for Finance, was staunchly opposed to reform and during a radio interview referred disparagingly to those involved as *"articulate, well-heeled middle class women."* Joan took the opportunity to address those comments while speaking on the Finance Bill a few days later in February 1978; *"I was appalled at the terminology used*

above Joan Burke, 1964
Courtesy of Ann Marie Burke Browne

opposite page Irish Independent, 1964
Courtesy of Irish Newspaper Archive

by the Minister for Finance in his weekend speech: "well-heeled, articulate women". Surely this was a slur on the whole female population. Does the Minister for Finance not realise that women too are playing their part in the economic life of the country? No doubt his expressions will be taken note of by the 51 per cent of the electorate and that 51 per cent includes Deputy Colley's well-heeled, articulate women. What was the slogan used by the Fianna Fáil Party prior to the last election? "Let us get the country moving". No doubt they have got the women moving but, if the remarks of the Minister for Finance are to be taken at their face value, then the country is moving backwards. I sincerely hope that that attitude of the Government will change, and change very quickly."

> "Women too are playing their part in the economic life of the country."

Consistently supportive of the rights of farmers, widows and nurses, Joan Burke drew extensively on her own experience in all three areas in her contributions on those issues in the Dáil. In 1978 she called for an inquiry into the remuneration and conditions of employment of nurses observing that; *"The nursing profession has been looked upon as the Cinderella profession of this country. Dedication and vocation are being exploited."* She often drew attention to the inadequate quality of the services available to those living in the West and during a speech on the financial resolutions of March 1980 she was scathing on the lack of progress being made by the Fianna Fáil Government;

"They are a Government elected with the biggest majority in our history who came to office committed to curb inflation and unemployment, to abolish car tax and rates on private houses and to give a subvention to the first-time buyers of new houses. The Government are composed of a party who did not acknowledge that there was a world economic recession between 1974 and 1977. They flatly rejected that the inflation in those years was due to external factors, dearer oil and dearer imported raw materials. During their two-and-a-half years in office they have not attempted to deliver the promises of the 1977 manifesto."

Joan Burke (née Crowley) was born in Bandon, Co. Cork on 8th February, 1928. She completed her secondary schooling at the Loreto in Killarney, then went to Dublin to train as a nurse. Joan initially trained as a fever nurse in Cherry Orchard, completing her general nursing studies in Galway. She later returned to Cherry Orchard where she worked as a nurse and then as a Sister. On her appointment to that post she was given a letter which said that she would have to forfeit her position if she got married.

Joan subsequently moved to Tulsk, Co. Roscommon on her marriage to Fine Gael TD and farmer James Burke. Following his untimely death in May 1964, Joan contested the Roscommon by-election which took place less than two months later. Despite the challenges inherent in running a farm and rearing two young children, she successfully served the people of Roscommon and Leitrim for seventeen years.

Joan was involved in a serious car accident in 1976, and the extent of the injuries she sustained led her to decline an offer of a junior ministry. Joan retired from politics in 1981. She passed away in 2016.

Joan Burke TD, 1964
Courtesy of Ann Marie Burke Browne

Throughout her time in the Dáil Joan Burke often advocated on behalf of widows, as evidenced by the following excerpt from a speech she made in 1971:

31 March 1971

Private Members' Business - Social Welfare Services for Widows and Orphans: Motion (Resumed)

Much has been said on this motion but surely it is a reflection on this House and this State that the plight of widows needs to be discussed? Perhaps one of the reasons for this is that this House has been dominated by men, who could not possibly understand or be expected to understand the financial problems which face many widows today. Added to the financial problems are the problems of loneliness and the change in social standing once the husband dies. When one realises that 75 per cent of our married women become widows one realises the size of the problem and the necessity for the Government and Members of this House to relieve the urgent and pressing financial difficulties that beset many of them.

We cannot lessen their grief but we can certainly help by easing the burden of worry and want. How could anyone exist on £4 10s a week plus 18s for the first two children and 13s for the third? Indeed the non-contributory pension is much worse, it is only £4 5s plus 15s for the first two children. With the ever-increasing cost of the essentials of life they could not possibly be expected to live on a miserable pension such as this.

Deputy Tully referred to the long delay in processing claims. A great deal of time is wasted from the time the application is made for a widow's pension until the final decision is made. It can very often take several months. These decisions could be expedited if the matter could be finalised at local level as a result of discussions with the local pension officers and the local social welfare officers and a provisional payment could be made.

Another problem which, thank goodness, does not happen very often is the case where a husband is killed and the authorities decide an inquest is necessary. It is very often nine or 12 months before the inquest is held and a death certificate cannot be issued until the inquest is over. Widow's pension cannot be paid until the death certificate has been issued.

The present widows' pensions are a false economy. Illness springs from undernourishment and mental anguish which are a direct result of the miserable allowances being paid to widows. I recently heard of a widow who had to abandon her children because she just could not cope any longer. No woman gives up her children easily and it must have taken something for this woman to give up her children and send them to an orphanage.

In conclusion I would like to ask the Minister to consider the position of widowers in poor circumstances because they too have to rear large families in some cases on their own.

PROUD TO SERVE: The Voices of the Women of Cumann na nGaedheal and Fine Gael 1922-1992

In one year her grocery bill has risen by 14%. But her housekeeping money hasn't.

DON'T BLAME THE GOVERNMENT
CHANGE IT!

The rising cost of living is one problem that has affected every single family in the country. On Wednesday there is one thing you can do to halt the vicious spiral. Vote Fine Gael.

The National Coalition Government is committed to dropping VAT from food. The outgoing government has resolutely refused to do so.

A vote for Fine Gael on Wednesday is to call a halt to rising prices. A vote for the outgoing government is a vote for continued rising prices.

Vote for a change.

VOTE FINE GAEL
Support the NATIONAL COALITION

PUBLISHED BY FINE GAEL

1957–1979 Shaping The Power of Politics For Women

> "I am sure the House will appreciate that there are many well educated, well intentioned women of integrity who would be ably equipped to perform the duty of serving as jurors."

1973 SENATOR
Mary Walsh

Senator 1973–1976

First female Chair of Wicklow County Council 1969–1970

First female Chair of the General Council of County Councils 1973

Fine Gael Director of Elections for Wicklow 1961

Member of Wicklow Vocational Education Committee for sixteen years

The first female Chair of Wicklow County Council, Mary Walsh was born in 1929 in Tinahely Co. Wicklow. She was educated at Loreto Abbey in Gorey before going on to study at University College Dublin (UCD) where she graduated with a Bachelor of Commerce (BComm) degree and a Higher Diploma in Education. A publican by trade, Mary owned and ran the Bridge House in Tinahely for many years until her sudden death in 1976, when the business was taken over by her brother and sister-in-law.

Mary joined Fine Gael and got actively involved in the local Party organisation. In 1960 she was elected to Wicklow County Council, and became the Party's local Director of Elections in 1961. She served as the first female Chair of Wicklow County Council in 1969 - 70, and was also the first woman elected to Chair the General Council of County Councils in 1973, a position she was again elected to in 1976.

Throughout her sixteen-year tenure as a member of Wicklow County Council, Mary served as a member of the Vocational Education Committee (VEC). She was an unsuccessful candidate in the 1970 Dáil election, and despite a good showing in the Seanad elections that year, failed to secure a seat. Again unsuccessful in the general election campaign of 1973 in Wicklow, Mary finally achieved her goal of entering national politics later that year when she was elected to the Cultural and Education Panel of the 13th Seanad. Her contributions to debates in Seanad Éireann included areas as diverse as social welfare, wildlife, juries, pollution and the licensing trade.

Mary's sudden death in 1976 shocked and saddened her many colleagues. The Fine Gael branch in Arklow was named after her for many years, while an educational bursary was awarded for almost thirty years in recognition of her interest in the educational welfare of young people. In his expressions of sympathy on her death in the Senate on 31st August, 1976, Cathaoirleach of the Seanad Senator James Dooge observed that;

Mary Walsh
Courtesy of of Paddy and Mary O'Toole

opposite page General Election ephemera, 1973
Courtesy of Alan Kinsella, Irish Election Literature

"Her speeches were always well-informed, forward-looking and thoughtful. Her death has taken from us a friend whose warm personality lightened the hearts of all who met her. Those who knew her could not fail to be aware of her untiring devotion to local government matters and to the interests of her constituents. Even more will they remember her great local patriotism, her love for her native county reflected in the enthusiasm with which she spoke of its beauties, and the vigour with which she spoke of the problems of the Wicklow people."

The following is an excerpt from Senator Mary Walsh's contribution on the second stage of the 1975 Juries Bill which refers to that year's Supreme Court finding that the 1927 Juries Act was unconstitutional.

4 February 1976

Juries Bill 1975, Second Stage

Like many other speakers who have spoken I, too, welcome this comprehensive legislation which in my opinion is long overdue. The widening of the scope of persons who can be appointed to serve as jurors is a welcome development. Under the 1927 Act liability for jury service was restricted mainly to the self-employed. This, for the most part meant small farmers or small-business-type persons. In a rural area, such as where I come from, this could have imposed a very great hardship because many of those people were not in a position to appoint others to carry on their businesses or farms in their absence, which sometimes was for as long as a week. In many instances they did not have the opportunity of serving as jurors. Nevertheless they were obliged to attend daily. Because very often the schedule of public transport did not facilitate them to be in attendance in court at the proper hours of sitting they found it necessary to hire taxis. If three or four persons went together and only one was called for service, this resulted in three or four men aimlessly ambling around the town for a day at considerable expense to themselves. I will not go into the other details but I think the Minister knows what I am referring to.

Sometimes it could be considered as a glorified holiday but I do not think the people at home considered it in that light. I know there are farmers who attended the spring sitting of the Circuit Court when, perhaps, they should have been putting in the crops. When it came to the autumn and the weather broke at harvest time they were often just that fortnight late in reaping the harvest. Many times the loss of the harvest was due to the fact that they were absent in, say, Wicklow at the Circuit Court when they should have been performing their own duties at home.

I had great reservations about the method in which jurors were summoned. I know the number of serving jurors was limited but at the same time there were instances of persons being called two years in succession. This created quite an amount of annoyance to the categories of people to whom I have referred.

"I too would have mixed feelings about certain categories of women serving as jurors. I refer particularly to married women with young children at home, or women who care for the sick or elderly, for whom jury service would create a very grave hardship."

I would like to refer to the Supreme Court decision in September regarding the virtual exclusion of women from jury service being unconstitutional. This is something which I welcome. I am sure the House will appreciate that there are many well educated, well intentioned women of integrity who would be ably equipped to perform the duty of serving as jurors.

On the other hand, I too would have mixed feelings about certain categories of women serving as jurors. I refer particularly to married women with young children at home, or women who care for the sick or elderly, for whom jury service would create a very grave hardship. These categories should be excusable under this new Act. Women who are pregnant may not have the stamina to serve for perhaps a week on a jury. This is another category which should be excusable.

There is also the question of the extension of the age limit from 65 to 70. While there are many retired people who would be able to serve on a jury, there are many others who suffer from heart ailments, diabetes and so on and for those jury service would create a grave hardship. Therefore, they should ipso facto be excusable as of right.

I am not completely in favour of a blanket extension of the age limit of 18 to 21. While that age group is eligible to vote and are in many instances capable and responsible, one needs experience of life before serving on a jury. I do not think a person in that age group would have the necessary experience. I refer in particular to civil cases such as car accidents where the jury member in the 18 to 21 age group might never have driven a car and would not be qualified to give the type of reasoned decision which many car accident cases entail.

Students are excusable under this Act but no mention has been made of the case of a post-primary student who is following an apprenticeship course on a day-release basis. These could be considered as part-time students and should be excusable as of right. The Minister has made provision for the payment of these students but they should be excusable because the loss of a week's study to serve as a juror might ultimately mean success or failure in a final examination.

PROUD TO SERVE: The Voices of the Women of Cumann na nGaedheal and Fine Gael 1922-1992

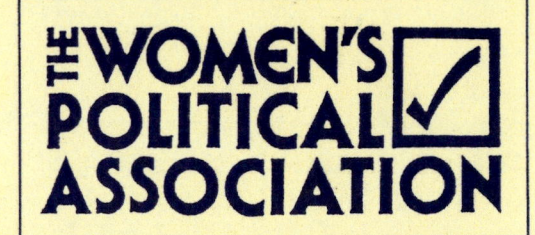

THE WOMEN'S POLITICAL ASSOCIATION ☑

MORE VOTES FOR YOUR WOMAN
WPA ☑
VOTE HER No. 1

AIM
To encourage, empower and promote the participation of women at all levels of public and political life.

Women's Political Association
Courtesy of Alan Kinsella, Irish Election Literature

1957–1979 Shaping The Power of Politics For Women

> *"I had to make sure that I stayed strong because you were conscious that if you made a mistake it would reflect on women generally."*

1977 SENATOR and TD
Gemma Hussey

Senator 1977-1981

Teachta Dála for Wicklow 1981-1982, 1982-1987, 1987-1989

First Female Minister for Education 1984

Minister for Social Welfare 1986-1987

Minister for Labour January–March 1987

Fine Gael Leader in the Seanad 1981-1982

The sole woman to sit at the Cabinet table from 1982-1987

Fine Gael spokesperson on Women's Affairs 1980-1981, Arts, Culture and Broadcasting 1982, Education 1987

Chair of the Women's Political Association

Gemma Hussey Election Literature 1981

Inspired by the women's movement and an adherence to liberal politics, Gemma Hussey joined the Women's Political Association in the 1970s. She was first elected as an independent Senator for the National University of Ireland in 1977, then joined Fine Gael in 1980, where she became the Party's leader in the Seanad from 1981 to 1982.

Gemma Hussey served as TD for her home constituency of Wicklow from 1982 to 1989 and in 1984 became the first woman to hold the position of Minister for Education. She also held the portfolio of Minister for Social Welfare between 1986 and 1987 and was Minister for Labour for a brief two-month period between January and March 1987. The sole woman to sit at the Cabinet table throughout the years 1982 to 1987, on her departure from politics Gemma Hussey set about working to help empower women to build movements for change in the former Eastern Bloc countries of Europe.

Two things inspired me to get into politics; the first was the women's movement and the second was a strong belief in liberal politics. Early on I was asked to join the Women's Political Association and I subsequently became its Chair. We went around the country attracting members, but we were fighting an uphill battle. Big meetings were rare, and I would have driven miles for an audience of four.

I ran for the NUI Senate as an independent in 1977 and became quite friendly with Dr Garret Fitzgerald. I very much liked his ideas of a pluralistic society and his constitutional crusade to liberalise Irish society. When I first joined Fine Gael, Garret wanted to make me Minister for Women's Affairs as a junior minister from the Senate. A deputation was quickly sent from the party backrooms to protest about promoting me over all the men in the Dáil, and that put paid to that.

There was a lot of jealousy and hidden sexism, *"Who does this one think she is?"* and all that kind of stuff. Garret himself was an instinctive feminist. I remember one discussion at cabinet about increasing social welfare rates and abolishing food subsidies. Jim Mitchell, a very nice man, said, "*Let's get some facts and figures here. Gemma, how much is a pound of rashers?*" And Garret said, "*Minister Mitchell, how would this woman know any more about the price of a pound of rashers than you do?*"

At the time Irish society was full of bias, things that we've almost forgotten now. When I got engaged my employer told me I had to resign, because I was getting married. Men got the children's allowance automatically, women couldn't get it and the legislation around violence in the home was really bad. Between 1982 and 1987 there wasn't a brass farthing in the country, but I managed to do an equalisation of social welfare payments and reduce some of the anomalies around gender. In Education, I introduced a system to make sure that examination papers didn't indicate whether a candidate was male or female. There was a certain amount of resistance to that, but the results showed that it changed things.

When I was Minister for Education Mary O'Rourke was opposition spokesperson and we both realised that if we started shouting at each other in the Dáil we would be immediately labelled "*harridans*", so we made a pact that we wouldn't get trapped by that kind of thing. There was one occasion where I'd won a point in debate across the floor and Mr. Haughey called me a vixen in the Dáil. I think even members of his own party were a bit shocked that he would use sexist language like that.

Leinster House is full of stories that this person had made a pass at some other person in the lift. That never happened to me, but I remember when Haughey was Minister for Health he brought out his family planning bill, "*An Irish Solution to an Irish Problem*". My supporters asked me to tell him that it wouldn't do, so I made an appointment to meet him. I went along to his offices in Leinster House, said my few words about the proposed bill and all the time he was looking me up and down in an unpleasant kind of way. Next thing he says, "*Now Gemma, let me say one thing to you. I know that the safe period wouldn't suit you any more than it would me.*" I couldn't believe what I was hearing. There was nobody else in the room and I didn't know what might happen next, so I just said; "*Well, I've said what I have to say*" and kind of stumbled out the door.

One of the first things I did in the Senate was to bring in a private members bill on rape. The question of marital rape had never been raised before, in fact there had been no legislation on rape, so I knew I was going to be using words that that were very difficult to say. I invited all my women supporters into the public gallery and every time I was coming to a difficult bit I looked over at them and it was fine. The bill passed unanimously in the Seanad, but the Government didn't accept it. Later, there was some other business going on in the Dáil chamber that I wanted to hear so I was sitting in the distinguished visitor's gallery. The next minute I felt a chuck on my bra strap. I leapt to my feet and there was Haughey behind me with a half-smile on his face. "*Just coming to tell you Senator, don't worry about your bill on marital rape. I'll see that through with the help of my very good new Minister for Justice Sean Doherty.*" I was completely taken aback. At that stage I was in my

"*Between 1982 and 1987 there wasn't a brass farthing in the country, but I managed to do an equalisation of social welfare payments and reduce some of the anomalies around gender.*"

Women's Political Association
Courtesy of Alan Kinsella, Irish Election Literature

thirties, new to the whole scenario and not an experienced politician. If I'd had more confidence I would have told him that was a disgrace. The more I think about those two incidents, the more I think that these stories deserve to be told.

In December 1982 the media kept ringing the late Nuala Fennell and myself to ask which woman should be in the Cabinet. I was furious when it turned out that there was only one woman and it was me for five years! I had to make sure that I stayed strong because you were conscious that if you made a mistake it would reflect on women generally. I didn't find it too bad except for the constant thing about how you look. That's always a problem for women. The nearest loo was two floors down, the men had a room next door to the Cabinet room, so there were various stupid things like that, but on the whole, I feel I held my own.

In each of the elections of that period I had a wonderful team of local Fine Gael supporters as well as a great team of friends who had been involved in the Women's Political Association. They would go out canvassing wearing their WPA stickers and I got into terrible trouble with the Party for introducing all these outsiders. My last election campaign was very difficult. Everybody thought I was going to be defeated. I blanketed the constituency with leaflets saying; *"You've got a great woman in Wicklow don't lose her"*. I won the seat; my running mate lost his and of course I was the worst in the world then.

During the 1983 abortion referendum the Party was split three ways. The Attorney General, Peter Sutherland, said that the referendum was ambiguous and dangerous and persuaded people to abstain, but it was a very bitter campaign. The things that people said and the kind of post you got! We were all exhausted by the end of it. I had some great friends. Katharine Bulbulia and Monica Barnes were terrific, but I remember sparks flying at a parliamentary party meeting during the divorce referendum. I stood up and said something and Alice Glenn pointed a finger across the room at me, *"Madam your day is done!"* She was a strong woman but very anti-liberal. I was always only sorry that Alice wasn't on our side.

I found the election of Mary Robinson absolutely exhilarating. When I go into Leinster House nowadays, it's great to see all the excellent women we have there that we didn't have before. I'm a great supporter of quotas because I saw what it achieved in other countries. I think women feel empowered by the recent referendum and what's needed now is concerted effort. Women won that referendum and I believe that all over the country now women are in the process of knowing how to win battles. They're going to go on winning battles and I think it's fantastic.

Divorce Referendum, 1986
Courtesy of Alan Kinsella,
Irish Election Literature

PROUD TO SERVE: The Voices of the Women of Cumann na nGaedheal and Fine Gael 1922-1992

Young Fine Gael National Conference, February 1979
Courtesy of Fine Gael

> "My main motivation for getting involved was that I strongly believed in the need for a just and caring society."

1979 TD
Myra Barry

Teachta Dála for Cork North East 1979–1981

Teachta Dála for Cork East 1981–1987

First Young Fine Gael member elected to the Dáil Fine Gael Spokesperson on Youth Affairs 1980–1982

Member of the Women's Rights Committee and the Joint Committee on Marriage Breakdown 1983

Motivated by a passion for a just and fair society, Myra Barry became a founding member of Young Fine Gael, helping to set up the Finglas branch of the organisation in the late 1970s. When she successfully contested the Cork North East by-election in 1979, she became the first Young Fine Gael member to be elected to the Dáil, heading the poll on her first outing. There were two by-elections in Cork on the same day and Fine Gael won both of them. The by-election results in his native county were one of the factors that led to the subsequent resignation of Jack Lynch as leader of Fianna Fáil.

Myra's father Richard was also a TD when Myra entered the Dáil, the only time to date that a parent and child have represented the same constituency in the same Dáil. She successfully contested three further elections, topping the poll on each occasion. Myra retired from politics in 1987.

I was born into politics. My parents met while canvassing and my father was a TD when I was born. My main motivation for getting involved was that I strongly believed in the need for a just and caring society. I would have been influenced by Declan Costello's *Towards A Just Society* and I was also a big fan of Garret Fitzgerald. His idealism and vision for a pluralist society was kind of infectious, and it seemed like a place where things could happen. I became a founding member of Young Fine Gael and we had a whole campaign around the abolition of illegitimacy. We were all very idealistic and enthusiastic, and we really believed we would make a difference and change things, not realising how slow change was.

When I stood in the by-election in 1979 I was just twenty-two and I really didn't think I had a chance of winning. I thought Fine Gael were giving me a run to see how I'd poll, and if I did well enough they might earmark me for the seat my father held when he retired. I remember there was a lot of energy around me,

Kerryman, 1979
Courtesy of Irish Newspaper Archive

Charlie McCreevy put a bet on me and I could feel the momentum gathering as the weeks went by. There were two by-elections that day and we weren't expecting to win either of them. Fianna Fáil always had the majority vote in the constituency, so it seemed unlikely that two TDs from the same house would be elected for Fine Gael. Liam Burke was running in Jack Lynch country, and nationally the Party had been down at heel after Fianna Fáil's 1977 auction politics manifesto, so those by-election wins were a big fillip in fortunes for Fine Gael.

At a personal level I made the transition into politics in the Dáil very easily. I quickly had a sense that I belonged and I loved representing the constituents. I found the Dáil chamber antiquated and adversarial. I brought a shopping basket into the Dáil on one occasion to signify the increase in basic grocery prices and the Ceann Comhairle told me I was not allowed bring visual aids into the chamber. At that time there were only about eight women there, it was very much a men's club and there were still some remnants of Civil War politics. For backbencher TDs there was no induction course, no research facilities and, as a backbencher, it was difficult to get heard in the Dáil, and making a difference was challenging. In terms of speaking times, the same unfairness still applies today for backbenchers from larger parties, but not from smaller parties. The reason I left in the end was because I didn't think that I was making a significant difference in terms of my aspirations towards a just society. The Dáil was a place where things changed very slowly and I felt I was a cog in the wheel of that system. It was like I could be doing this for the next fifty years and would it change society that much? A lot of much needed Dáil reform has only started to occur in recent years. I had headed the poll in the by-election and in three general elections so people were wondering how I could walk away from it, but actually Garret was very understanding at the time.

The maiden speech was a big thing. I was due to speak just before the Dáil finished for the night, but someone went on and on and my turn didn't come. When I told my father he said, "It's a pity now, when you go in there in the morning you'll have the whole house looking at you, including the Taoiseach". The next morning after the order of business the Taoiseach usually leaves and I asked Charlie Haughey to stay and listen to me as he obviously didn't understand young people and if he'd just sit down and listen he might learn something. He sat down and clapped when I had finished. That's what made the headlines the next day; "Taoiseach claps for maiden speech".

Communication systems were very different then. We were in the era of handwritten letters and I remember getting a telegram from Sean Barrett saying, "Be in the Dáil tomorrow." There was also a real vacuum around information, whereas now, with all the information available on the internet, you could do a lot of that research from your office.

My memory is that it was very hard for women. Some women got a hard time from some of the men when they'd try to push the "Women's Agenda", and the idea that women had a rightful role in politics and were entitled to be there. There were some snide comments and even trying to change things like the languaging

"I am hopeful when I see all the Fine Gael women around the country."

of parliamentary party meetings was difficult. Looking back, the men never gave me a hard time. I think because I was mixing with rural TDs across the parties they would have regarded me very much as part of the pack, and because I was young they would have been protective of me. I don't ever remember feeling put down by them, or that I didn't belong or "who did I think I was saying that?" I did have the sense that I was being treated equally. It was like being a member of the club, that each one of us was elected to this assembly democratically and everybody knew how hard it was to get elected, and there was a sense of mutual respect for that.

The 1983 referendum campaign was very stressful and I think it was the only time in my political career that I told a journalist I was putting the phone down because he was accusing me of being a murderer. It was nasty and vicious. After all these years I still remember vividly the confusion the day Peter Sutherland came into the parliamentary party meeting and advised us the wording of the proposed Eighth Amendment to the Constitution was unsatisfactory and everything got turned on its head. I think one of the mistakes we made as politicians around some of the more socially divisive campaigns of the 1980s and '90s involved sticking to the adversarial British system of politics we inherited. This time people seemed much more respectful of each other's opinions and I think the Citizen's Assembly was a good idea. That's probably one of the good things about the new politics, everything doesn't have to be black or white.

I'm humbled and honoured that the people of East Cork put their faith in me at such a young age. I'm proud that Fine Gael has always been the party of social change and that we managed to turn the economy around at a time when unemployment was 18%, as we did again in more recent times. I also think that Young Fine Gael has been a good vehicle for young people outside political families to get involved in politics. Back then, I would have thought that women would have made a breakthrough without quotas, but actually now I realise that they were needed.

I am conscious that politics is continuously challenging and the maintenance of female TDs in the Dáil will require supports such as maternity leave, appropriate crèche facilities etc., especially for female rural deputies. What you're learning is that the challenges are all quite individualistic, so you have to build different systems for different needs. I am hopeful when I see all the Fine Gael women around the country and the current crop of women in the Dáil, who all seem very able and confident that there is a great future for women in politics. I think society as a whole will benefit from the increased participation of women in Dáil Eireann and increased gender balance in the years ahead.

Fine Gael women TDs elected in 1982.
Gemma Hussey, Alice Glenn, Nuala Fennell, Mary Flaherty,
Nora Owen, Avril Doyle, Madeleine Taylor-Quinn, Monica Barnes and Myra Barry.
Image courtesy of Sarah Barnes

1981–1992
Pushing Politics to Deliver Rights For Women

> "The way we organise business in this House is a disgrace. I regret that the five minutes in which I have to speak will be the only contribution from a woman Member."

1981 TD and SENATOR
Nuala Fennell

Teachta Dála for Dublin South 1981-1987

Senator 1987

Teachta Dála for Dublin South 1989-1992

Minister of State at the Department of the Taoiseach with responsibilities for Women's Affairs and Family Law 1982-1987

Fine Gael Frontbench Spokesperson on Women's Affairs 1982

Member of the Women's Rights Committee 1987-1989; 1989-1992

Spokesperson on Health 1989-1992

Founding member of AIM, ADAPT and Women's Aid

The first Woman President of the European Association of Former Parliamentarians

Nuala Fennell first came to public prominence through her activism and leadership in the area of women's rights during the 1970s. In keeping with societal norms for married Irish women at the time, Nuala had to give up work after the birth of the first of her three children, becoming as she put it, *"One of the foot soldiers in the vast army of suburban housewives in the 1960s and 1970s"*. Writing about that time in her 2009 memoir *Political Woman*, Nuala recalled; *"I felt invisible, irrelevant and in a role from which I wanted escape. Not escape from Brian and the children whom I loved dearly, but from the domestic cell of tedious repetition and the sense of being brain dead. For me it was stop the world I want to get on"*.

Nuala began questioning the way in which Irish women were *"segregated into very specific roles which appeared irredeemably fixed"*. She began to write articles for the women's pages of Irish newspapers and through her efforts discovered *"a large audience of women who felt equally frustrated and impatient with their lives"*. Her writing also brought her into contact with the journalist Mary Kenny who persuaded her to attend her first meeting of the Irish Women's Liberation Movement. Nuala helped produce *Irish Women: Chains or Change*, a report which outlined the widespread discrimination suffered by women under the Irish Constitution and the legal system. The document proposed an agenda for change based on five key action points; "Equal pay, equality before the law, equal education opportunities, contraception and justice for deserted wives, widows and unmarried mothers."

In the years following the demise of the Irish Women's Liberation Movement, Nuala's commitment to securing change in each of these areas led her to found organisations including AIM, an education and advocacy group spearheading change in family law reform and ADAPT (Association for Deserted and Alone Parents). Nuala helped establish the Women's Refuge in Dublin in 1974 and became the first Chair of Women's Aid a year later. She also joined the Women's Political Association.

Nuala's first foray into national politics entailed running a 'DIY election campaign' as an independent candidate in the 1977 general election, in which she performed well but didn't get elected. In 1978 she joined Fine Gael and while her first outing as a party candidate in the European elections of 1979 didn't result in a seat, she was elected as TD for Dublin South in June 1981. Her Dáil maiden speech dealt with some of the concerns of Irish women at that time, including health and maternity needs, supporting women to re-enter the workforce and updating family law. On her re-election in February 1982, Nuala became Fine Gael Frontbench Spokesperson on Women's Affairs and following the November 1982 election was appointed Minister of State at the Department of the Taoiseach (with responsibilities for Women's Affairs and Family Law).

Nuala's stewardship in the role was impressive. Two important equality acts concerning domicile and citizenship rights were passed, while 1986 saw the establishment of the Family Mediation Service. A successful Women in Business initiative was also piloted that year and Nuala steered the landmark legislation on the abolition of illegitimacy through the Seanad and the Dáil before the 1987 general election. When she lost her seat, Taoiseach Garret Fitzgerald appointed her to the 17th Seanad. She was then elected to the Labour Panel in the 18th Seanad and returned to the Dáil in 1989 where she served as Junior Health Spokesperson and was a member of the Joint Committee on Women's Rights.

Much of her childhood was spent in Portlaoise where her father was stationed as a Garda Sergeant. On the family's return to Dublin, Nuala was educated at the Dominican College, Eccles Street, where she completed a secretarial course and secured a job in a tea importing firm on Bachelor's Walk. She met her future husband Brian Fennell, and the couple travelled to Canada in 1957 where they lived in Montreal. On their return to Ireland, they married and Nuala got a job as a legal secretary.

Following her retirement from national politics in 1992, Nuala ran Political Communications, a public relations company. She was also one of the founders and first president of the Irish Parliamentary Society, an organisation for former TDs and Senators. She subsequently became the first Woman President of the European Association of Former Parliamentarians. Nuala's memoir *Political Woman* was published shortly after her death in 2009.

The following excerpt is taken from a speech given by Nuala Fennell during her final term in the Dáil.

8 July 1992

Health (Family Planning) (Amendment) Bill 1992 Second Stage

I deplore the haste with which this legislation is being brought in. It is very difficult for someone like me who has a long term interest in this subject because I had to make my views known in the "letters to the editor" column. The way we organise business in this House is a disgrace. I regret that the five minutes in which I have to speak will be the only contribution from a woman Member. The lack of family planning grievously affects women.

The whole debate is furtive, it is as if we are ashamed of what we are doing here. This is only the third time that family planning has been discussed in this House, in 1979, 1985 and today. Members should think about the message this debate is sending out, it is a message that it is something shameful, which we cannot discuss openly or debate honestly. It is restricted in the most dreadful way. We are in the medieval age with regard to contraception. It is regrettable that the Minister for Health, who I am convinced cares and knows better, has not had the courage and leadership to go all the way and to have a proper debate. We do not need laws, we need to provide information, facilities and to ensure that everyone who is sexually active has a responsible attitude to family planning.

If we are to have a debate it should be an open, honest one. Let us look at the total area of family planning and the needs in relation to it. We should take account of the awful circumstances from January of this year in relation to the High Court and Supreme Court cases on the young woman who was raped and subsequently became pregnant. That is part of this debate and we are very remiss in having such a limited and small section in this Bill and leaving out all the other areas. I should like to have the area of information discussed; the Minister missed a wonderful opportunity to amend the 1979 Act to enable us to have proper information outlets and policies with regard to family planning and, if necessary, abortion referral.

I stress the need to change the whole approach to family planning from the medical approach. Far too many Irish women are on the pill. Many women who would not have access to family planning clinics or to GPs who would have a sympathetic approach to all forms of family planning will tend to take the pill. In many instances this is very bad for them. Problems like varicose veins or other medical conditions may arise. There should be a promotion campaign to inform men and women about the various forms of contraception, where they can get them and what is safe for them. The thrust of the Bill to make condoms more readily available is right but we must go much further. Condoms are readily available and their use does not interfere with a person's physical state. They have been proved to be effective.

> "The lack of family planning grievously affects women."

I join with other speakers on this side of the House who have condemned the age limit and have suggested that it is ludicrous not to allow condoms to be sold through slot machines. The sky will not fall if we agree to give people freedom of choice by allowing slot machines. We should let individuals make their own decisions. What will happen to the eleven slot machines which are already in position? Are the Garda Síochána to be deployed, when the Bill is passed, to take away these slot machines? That question must be answered, given the explicit condition in the Bill.

I would ask for greater information on the availability of family planning. I have in mind information which would be provided by the Department of Health. I asked some time ago what information is available to people who want to know the various forms of family planning. I was referred by the Department of Health to the Mother and Child Book, a delightful book published for young mothers to tell them about feeding their babies and the first developmental steps. That is an inappropriate response to somebody who inquires about family planning. I would hope that we would reach maturity.

We will not get the chance, during this furtive and hasty debate, to educate and inform people, to tell them that they are perfectly entitled to plan their family and to adopt a responsible approach to sex if they are sexually active, so that children who are not wanted are not conceived and we can reduce the number of women going abroad for abortions and the huge number of children conceived outside marriage, most of whom are not wanted and end up in the deprived zone of society, poor, uneducated and without a proper chance in life. I would wish for a fuller debate and a more generous and open approach to this legislation. One must welcome it as a means of improving the awful position which exists but it does not go far enough.

Fine Gael General Election ephemera

PROUD TO SERVE: The Voices of the Women of Cumann na nGaedheal and Fine Gael 1922-1992

Madeline Taylor-Quinn . . . "I would like to be a minister".

Picture by AIDAN O'KEEFFE

Sunday Independent, 1991
Courtesy of Irish Newspaper Archive

1981–1992 Pushing Politics to Deliver Rights For Women

> *"My starting point was always about fairness."*

1981 TD and SENATOR
Madeleine Taylor-Quinn

Teachta Dála for Clare
1981-1982, 1982-1987
1987-1989, 1989-1992

Senator 1982-1982, 1992-1997
1997-2002

The first female TD for the constituency of Clare

Chair of the Select Committee on Judicial Separation

Spokesperson on Marine, Defence and European Security 1987–1992

In the Seanad she served as Deputy Leader, Spokesperson on Foreign Affairs, Justice and Law Reform

Member of the National Economic and Social Forum and the National Forum for Europe

First Fine Gael Mayor of Clare

As a young teenager, Madeleine Taylor made speeches in churches throughout her native Co. Clare when her father Frank ran for election in 1969. She later went on to set up a branch of Young Fine Gael in Kilrush, and another in UCG when she was a student in Galway. She was the first person to hold the position of Honorary Secretary outside the parliamentary party, as well as a member of the provisional Young Fine Gael executive in the late 1970s.

On her election to Dáil Éireann in 1981, Madeleine became County Clare's first female TD. Having lost her seat in February 1982, she was elected to the Cultural and Educational Panel of Seanad Éireann and then regained her Dáil seat at the November 1982 general election. She held her seat at the 1987 and 1989 general elections and served on the Fine Gael Frontbench from 1987-1992 as Spokesperson on Marine, Defence and European Security. She was elected to Seanad Éireann on the Cultural and Educational Panel in 1992 and held her seat until 2002. While in the Seanad she served as Deputy Leader, Spokesperson on Foreign Affairs, Justice and Law Reform.

In 2004 she contested the European Elections in the Ireland North-West Constituency when Clare was merged with Connaught/Ulster. She polled way beyond Party expectations with 43,400 votes, thus securing the Fine Gael seat for Jim Higgins which was under threat from Sinn Féin. During her time in national politics Madeleine spent six years on the Fine Gael front bench, serving on committees including Women's Rights, Foreign Affairs, the National Economic and Social Forum and the National Forum for Europe. Following her election and serving as first Fine Gael Mayor of Clare, she retired from Clare County Council in 2009 following thirty years as a public representative.

I had this wonderful, naïve view that if you got actively involved in the political system you could actually forge change in society. In my latter teenage years, I was particularly concerned about the poverty I saw around parts of rural Clare. I thought the treatment of women who got pregnant outside marriage was wrong, and the way children born outside wedlock were treated was appalling. People claimed to have all these great Christian principles, but they were applying none of them to children. My starting point was always about fairness, so the first thing I did when I was in Young Fine Gael was to get a motion passed to abolish the status of illegitimacy. Subsequently, I was in a position to give things a final push and help Nuala Fennell get the legislation over the line before we were out of government in 1987.

I stood successfully for the County Council elections in 1979 and then when the 1981 election came up, Peter Prendergast was pushing me to go. I wasn't really ready, but I got elected. There was another election very soon afterwards and I lost my seat. Subsequent to that, I was beginning to get strange things being said to me. When I pursued it further, I discovered that one of the planks used to get me off the pitch was a rumour that I had been caught for drunken driving and had gone to England for an abortion at Christmas.

At the next convention, I was midway through making my selection speech, when I decided to address the issue; "During the course of the last election a lot of character assassination comments were made about me. I know where they originated, I know that they've infiltrated into parts of Fine Gael and there are people here tonight who also spread that rumour. If I hear a scintilla of character assassination about me during the course of this campaign I will take the person who propagates it to whatever court sits the following morning." While I was saying all this there was absolute silence in the hall. There were about eight hundred people there that evening, and afterwards not one person asked me what I was talking about. That, to me, was the biggest shock. It was much wider known than I had realised, and nobody had said it to me.

That election saw a seismic shift in the political scene of Clare. Fine Gael got two seats and Donal Carey and myself were like some kind of pin-up novelties. To finally break the mould in the home of De Valera politics was like manna from heaven. After that it was eighteen hours a day, seven days a week. The country was in a dire economic situation, we were hanging on by one vote in government and it was vicious on the ground, because Fianna Fáil wanted their seats back in Clare. That was all very difficult, but you just learned to battle.

We had the divorce referendum, the abortion referendum, the condom legislation, what should have been just normal, but what was extraordinary abnormal at the time. I was on the moderate liberal side of the Party and what you'd have to listen to during those parliamentary party debates was confounding. The debate on illegitimacy was particularly savage. There was huge opposition to it, they were all going to lose their farms and their businesses, and I remember saying that there must be an awful lot of lads with lots of extra-curricular activities, judging by the nature of the debate.

I remember I was eight months pregnant during the '83 referendum. SPUC were ruthless, sending deputations of priests, parish priests and monsignors,

"Public service is a privilege but there's no place for someone who thinks there's going to be a soft, easy furrow to election."

threatening you with your seat, and the stuff that was coming through the post would make you throw up. One Sunday I went to mass in Ennis cathedral and the priest started to ramble on about the referendum. I walked out, went across to the Old Ground Hotel, rang the Bishop and we had about an hour of an altercation on the phone. It shows you the dominance of the church, and the patriarchal society that we were operating in at the time. I think the last referendum has put paid to that.

I loved the cut and thrust of parliamentary politics, the debate, the fine combing and analysis of bills. I pushed a lot of issues and I chaired the Select Committee on Judicial Separation. Getting that through was very significant because it was the foundation for the divorce referendum and there was a lot of resistance to it, particularly from some of the Fianna Fáil representatives. Another thing I found in the course of constituency work was that if a woman with land married a farmer they could only have one herd number, and her herd number always had to be subsumed into his. I brought that to the Women's Committee and we succeeded in changing that, just a little bit of fair play again. Locally, Clare Care were refused a grant from the Department of Health to buy a property to set up an alcoholic treatment unit. I brought a deputation to meet the senior officials and we put a very strong case. We got the decision overturned and there is a fantastic treatment centre there now.

Public service is a privilege but there's no place for someone who thinks there's going to be a soft, easy furrow to election. There's a lot to learn and you can't represent people if you have no understanding of where they're coming from and what their issues are. The council is an essential foot step to the Dáil, in rural areas particularly. It's a baptism of fire but you're getting an understanding of people, situations, inequalities, and the things that need to be changed. I had to put in an awful lot of groundwork in Clare and in Fine Gael nationally before I was elected to anything. There is a very selective misconception out there in relation to being handed the seat. Nobody would have referred to Garret Fitzgerald being handed a seat, yet his father was there before him. You don't get a seat without fighting for it.

I was aware of the hesitancy that existed within the organisation around electing a woman. You had to be much more careful of everything you did, and I knew that I had to show myself to be really competent, in a way that a man wouldn't have had to. I never found hostility from the men in the Party organisation in Clare. They were generally always supportive and came out to canvass. There wouldn't have been as many women involved, but the older women were really pleased to have a woman to vote for. It was like a new dawn for them.

Women around an issue can be a powerful force, but until you get more of a body of women involved in the organisation, you can't possibly have as many women coming to the surface in conventions, despite the quota. As women we were part of a change and our presence brought a different view point into Dáil and parliamentary party discussions on many issues. You wouldn't be even aware sometimes of where you were making an impact. Monica was a real trailblazer and Alice Glenn was dogged in her way of thinking but she shows the diversity of voices that existed at that time. There were highs and lows, but it was a privilege and it was entertaining and hopefully we did some good along the way.

Govt. must tackle poverty, Mulrany F.G. members told

It was estimated that one in four of all Irish people were living in poverty and of them, retired people, women and farmers topped the list, said Mrs. Mary Flaherty, Minister of State, Departments of Health and Social Welfare in Mulrany on Friday.

Ms. Flaherty told guests at the annual Dinner of Mulrany Fine Gael Branch the Government was acutely aware of the problem of poverty.

"Poverty comes in many different forms, but knows no boundaries or class barriers," she said. "I believe that a major public education programme is required to show the extent to which a large number of people in Ireland today are living at a level which most of us would find unacceptable."

The main groupings are — on a 1972 survey were:

- **The Elderly**
  Indications are that up to 40% of retired households, i.e., where the head of the house is retired, are 'poor.' This is particularly the case where elderly females are living alone.
- **The Unemployed**
  Approximately 10% of the unemployed households, i.e., where head of the house is unemployed, are living in poverty.
- **The Sick**
  Almost 6% of households where the head of the house is out of work because of illness live in poverty.
- **The Low Paid**
  17% of households among the lower paid are living n poverty.
- **Large Families**
  Households with a large number of children (5 or more) account for almost 12% of all poor households.
- **The Disabled**
  While disabled persons do not in themselves account for a large portion of our poor population, they are very much at risk.
- **Farmers**
  Farm households accout for over 20% of the poor.
- **Women**
  Overall, women in this country account for almost 33% of our poor, including the elderly, widows and deserted wives.
- **Single Parents**
  This again would amount to a small percentage but a group very much at risk.

Ms. Flaherty urged: "We must assess and discover a great deal more about the effectiveness of the social welfare system in helping these households and why some groups and not others are relieved from the suffering of poverty.

COMMITMENT

"The Government must tackle the problem of poverty in a sustained and planned way. My appointment as Minister of State with responsibility for the alleviation of poverty is a clear indication of our commitment in this direction.

"Initially it is my intention to draw up an anti-poverty plan within the context of national and social planning. Since my appointment I have been briefing myself on the overall situation. I wish to move carefully on re-establishing the Combar Poverty programme to ensure that the lessons learned are incorporated into any new programmes. Additionally, wider programmes than any so far envisaged may be needed," she added.

John and Christine Kelly, Ennis, Miss Mary Flaherty, T.D., Margaret and Seamus McLoughlin, Claremorris were at the Mulrany Fine Gael Dinner in the Great Western Hotel.

Western Journal, 1981
Courtesy of Irish Newspaper Archive

> "Finglas was a very challenging place for Fine Gael people in the 70s when Fianna Fáil and the Labour Party dominated."

1981 TD
Mary Flaherty

Teachta Dála for Dublin North West 1981–1997

Minister of State at the Departments of Health and Social Welfare 1981 Portfolios on the Fine Gael Front Bench include Health 1987, Overseas Development 1988, Social Welfare 1989–1990, Energy 1990–1993 and Labour Affairs 1993

Member of National Executive of Young Fine Gael

Founder Member and first Secretary of the Young Fine Gael branch in Finglas

Galvanised by the election defeat of 1977, Mary Flaherty joined Young Fine Gael and helped found a local branch of the organisation in her native Finglas. Later elected to the National Executive of Young Fine Gael, she became actively involved in the campaign to save Wood Quay and won a seat on Dublin City Council in 1979. Two years later she was elected TD for Dublin North West, and much to her surprise, was appointed Minister of State at the Department of Social Welfare by Taoiseach Garret Fitzgerald on her first day in the Dáil.

During that six month tenure as junior minister she frequently deputised for Minister Eileen Desmond who was then very ill. That entailed mastering a complex portfolio encompassing the work of two government departments, and in the years that followed, Mary also undertook a number of roles on the Fine Gael front bench. She married Fine Gael TD Alderman Alexis Fitzgerald in 1982 and the couple had four children. Mary represented the constituency of Dublin North West continuously until her defeat at the 1997 general election, and after her time in national politics she spent nineteen years as CEO of the children's charity CARI.

> I thought the 1973 - 1977 government was a brilliant, reforming coalition that began the transformation of Irish society, particularly for women. When it was wiped out by a giveaway budget I was so angry that I felt I had to get involved. In a strange way that defeat both activated me and gave me the opportunity, because Garret became leader and established Young Fine Gael, which was really my gateway to activity.
>
> We set up a local branch of Young Fine Gael and it was an interesting time in the Party with the Just Society versus the more conservative view. I was firmly in the social democratic mode and I would have liked to see the Party go much

more in that direction. I got very involved with the Wood Quay issue and that's how I met my husband Alexis. He was an Alderman on the Council at the time, in favour of the conservation of Wood Quay, and he was the person picked by Peter Prendergast to take me aside and ask me to run for the locals.

Finglas was a very challenging place for Fine Gael people in the 70s when Fianna Fáil and the Labour Party dominated, but it was known that I was teaching locally, and that my mother was a midwife who had delivered two and a half thousand babies. They were all then of voting age and there was a good chance that Nurse Flaherty's daughter would get preferences down the line. Initially I was thinking I'd wait until I got settled down, but then the constituency boundaries were redrawn, and there was nobody representing my side of the Party in the area where I lived. I got through the convention and I remember the Women's Political Association was very strong back then. They had these great little yellow stickers with the slogan "Vote for your woman" and I took the only Fine Gael seat on the council that time. The incumbent Paddy Belton, had been a proponent of the building on Wood Quay and he said afterwards, "Women and Wood Quay beat me."

The City Council was really satisfying, I loved the work and I got very involved in practical things, education, general purposes and later on the cultural side with the Hugh Lane Gallery. I was asked to chair the Young Fine Gael campaign for the abolition of the Status of Illegitimacy. I was lucky with the mentoring and support I got in the beginning from people of the calibre of Peter Prendergast and Dan Egan. There was good strategic thinking and understanding at a central organisational level then, and it was possibly the weakness of that in later years that may have resulted in the loss of my seat. Roll on five Dáil elections, a number of local elections and you get tired, and then you get somebody who is ambitious and wants to run against you. In my case I think there was bad judgement in headquarters. The most marginal seat in the country was Dublin North West and it was not traditional Fine Gael heartland. I may have lost it anyway, but that last convention was held very early and I had to accept a running mate, who passed me out by a hundred votes and didn't manage to hold the seat for the Party.

When I was first elected to the Dáil I had six months as a junior minister at the Department of Health and Social Welfare with Special Responsibility for Poverty and Family Welfare. I wasn't expecting it, and it led to huge jealousy, some expressed openly, some of which I heard about afterwards. My minister, Eileen Desmond, was very ill, I had to do a lot of Dáil questions, and it meant learning very quickly. There was also a lot of focus on me as a young woman and on my clothes. There were a couple of very nasty social journalists at the time, and they used to try and get a picture of me in my Merc and call me the Minister for Poverty. That intrusive, personal side was very hard, so when I stopped being minister there was a real desire to just disappear for a while and build up my basic constituency work, and I did that for a period of years as I also started my family.

I would have been a moderate on the social issues and I remember a discussion on abortion at one Ard Fheis where I was asked, "*Now what do you think Mary?*" You're inching your way on a complex debate and I said, "*I don't think they should

"I wrote the party's first policy on Development Aid. Fine Gael was the first party to commit to the target of 0.7% aid."

be treated as criminals". The headline afterwards was, "*Flaherty for legalization of abortion*". I think there's been an interesting development of the structures in the Dáil and in society that have also allowed the debate to mature in the years since, but that was an impossible time. Not only were people finding the issues difficult, but the economic background was chaotic and there was an anger that so much time was being taken up with social issues. The Labour Party had agreed to come into power on the basis of a 3% increase in social welfare and because inflation was 22% and interest rates were 15%, we had to give a 25% increase in social welfare. Life was unbelievably hard, and I think Garret's exceptional energy and talent was divided. That may also have exhausted him, which lead to him quitting in 1987, rather than staying around to re-group.

After that period as a junior minister I had a series of front bench roles. I took over Nora Owen's work on development when she lost her seat in 1987, and I wrote the Party's first policy on Development Aid. Fine Gael was the first party to commit to the target of 0.7% aid, so that was very satisfying. Within the committee system we did a lot of hard work amending draft legislation including pensions bills. At that time, it was against regulations for teachers to hit children, but it wasn't against the law, so we made that change in the committee. In my constituency you can see the results of practical decisions you were involved in, whereas at Dáil level unless you get some periods in government it can be hard to see tangible results, although I have to say, the development of the committee system has helped. You see all those wonderful women that have come in now in Fine Gael and Noel Rock finally getting the seat back in North West after nineteen years was just fantastic.

Maybe because of my own internal qualities I didn't feel inhibited because of being a woman. I had one approach in the inappropriate behaviour category but in those days you just took that as grist to the mill and waved them off. John Kelly told me once he used to believe that there wasn't a place for women in law or politics, but later he said he thought we added to the tone and quality of the debate, and reduced some of the macho manoeuvrings that went on.

My first instinct in saying I'd wait until I was settled might have been correct, but it was a great career and it happened organically for me. I found that the only big inhibitor for me eventually was family and combining the two. People like Monica and Nuala came in when their children were older, whereas I got elected before I had my first child. One and two children are manageable, but when you get to three and four it's extremely difficult. We had various kinds of childcare and Alexis was good when his political career ended, but you're always compromising, rushing away from things to get back, so that became a big factor in your capacity to grow yourself as a politician.

I think women have to take family into account and really plan around it, but if they really want women involved in politics I think there has to be some sort of weighting. Some of the European models achieve a mix by having a number of directly elected and a quota that allows you to fill other gaps, so maybe list rather than quota, but having been there and watched it, I don't think there's much else stopping women.

PROUD TO SERVE: The Voices of the Women of Cumann na nGaedheal and Fine Gael 1922-1992

"*That's an excellent suggestion, Miss Triggs. Perhaps one of the men here would like to make it.*"

Courtesy of Punch Magazine Ref: 1988.01.08.11

1981–1992 Pushing Politics to Deliver Rights For Women

"I was an anonymous suburban housewife who hadn't been in the reckoning at all, so I feel I was elected in my own right."

1981 TD
Nora Owen

Teachta Dála for Dublin North 1981-1982, 1982-1982, 1982-1987, 1989-1992, 1992-1997, 1997-2002

First female Deputy Leader of Fine Gael 1993

Minister for Justice 1994–1997

Chair of the Joint Committee on Cooperation with Developing Countries 1986

Vice-Chair of the Foreign Affairs Committee

Nora Owen was deeply involved in her community and busy raising three children when the local branch of Fine Gael approached her to run for a seat in the local elections of 1979. As a councillor Nora quickly established a reputation as a "go-to" person around local issues. One of her very first campaigns was about the impact of the venomous "Malahide Mosquito", a public health issue which was adversely affecting people's lives in the area at the time.

At that stage, despite a lineage that included having two TDs in the family (her uncle Sean and her grandaunt Margaret Collins-O'Driscoll), as well as being the grandniece of Michael Collins, Nora hadn't considered getting involved in national politics. Then in 1981 a general election was called and the addition of twenty-one new seats resulted in a concerted effort to get new people elected. Nora was first returned to the Dáil in 1981, successfully retaining her seat in a second election in February 1982, and then again in November 1982. Having lost her seat in 1987, she returned to the Dáil in 1989, and continued to be returned until losing her seat in the general election of 2002. Highlights of her political career include representing her constituency for almost two decades, becoming Deputy Leader of Fine Gael in 1993 and serving as Minister for Justice from 1994 - 1997. She is the sister of former Fine Gael MEP Mary Banotti.

The year I was first elected coincided with the breakthrough of women in Irish politics. Up until 1981 the majority of women in the Dáil were widows or daughters of deceased or former members and between the various elections of the early 1980s we got people like Monica Barnes, Nuala Fennell and Gemma Hussey elected for Fine Gael. That was Garret's influence I think, and also good management by the Secretary General of the Party Peter Prendergast. By 1987 there were campaigns like "Why not a woman?" but while there was a good voice for women in the parliamentary party we also had quite a right-wing section. The debate on the 1983 amendment was very fraught, particularly after we got Peter Sutherland's advice on the wording. At that time about twenty-one of us were adamantly against it and we were able to abstain in the Dáil. Only Alan Shatter and Monica Barnes broke the whip.

I remember nearly all the women spoke in favour of the decriminalisation of homosexuality, because we were used to being discriminated against. There was a time when a woman over forty couldn't get a permanent teaching job, as my own mother discovered when my father died. There were other things too, like the fact that a man could get a tax allowance to hire a woman to mind the children if his wife died, whereas a woman who had been widowed couldn't. We had to open doors, there's no two ways about it.

For a long time, the Party Chair was always a man and as a minority in the room you had to make sure you got heard. I remember keeping a cartoon of a meeting pinned to my noticeboard. In it there were a number of men and one woman around a table and the caption read; "Well Miss Triggs, that was a very good suggestion. Now perhaps one of the men would like to make it." That experience was quite typical. At meetings you could often be ignored until somebody else brought the same thing up, so you had to be quite assertive. Then, of course, you'd get called bossy and have things like "Oh for God's sake!" being said to you.

That first election to the Dáil was very tough. All through the campaign I was listening to the radio and they'd be saying things like; "We hear that the second Fine Gael candidate seems to be doing well." They never gave my name and I used to shout; "Say my name please!" It was the same when I attended the election count at Ballymun Comprehensive School with my sister Mary. They never referred to me as Nora; it was always "she" or "our second candidate". One of the journalists said, rather rudely, "It looks like you're going to get elected and we don't seem to have very much information about you." I said, "Well I suppose it's time you began to learn."

We won the seat by a handful of votes. It hadn't been factored in, but it ended up being the one that got us into government. Shortly afterwards one of the journalists was overheard ringing his paper reading out his piece; "An anonymous suburban housewife has just had a surprise victory in Dublin North." One of my workers was passing and he said, "She's not anonymous!" and the poor fellow got very flustered. Essentially though, I was an anonymous suburban housewife who hadn't been in the reckoning at all, so I feel I was elected in my own right.

There is no training course to be a TD. You bring your life's experience and you learn on-the-job and I would say to any woman who is interested, take the opportunities. You will be scared, you'll want to go to the bathroom three times before you stand up at a public meeting or speak in the Dáil, but then suddenly you'll find your voice. The other thing that women TDs with children have to do is arrange to have them minded. My husband Brian did the lion's share of that for most of the time I was in the Dáil, but I also hired a full-time housekeeper.

> "All through the campaign I was listening to the radio and they'd be saying things like; "We hear that the second Fine Gael candidate seems to be doing well." They never gave my name and I used to shout; 'Say my name please!'"

I was able to do the school run in the morning and knowing that Esther was with the boys when they came in from school meant that I didn't have to worry. There's always an interest in what women are wearing and how they look tends to be criticised more than how a man looks. I used to get my makeup done professionally when I was a minister, particularly if I was going to Brussels at 6am and while it sounds vain, it's really about your own confidence, so women need to be aware of these things.

I think women's antagonism to politics is around the adversarial side of it. When I was Minister for Justice I got some tough times from my opposite number John O'Donoghue, but I used to use a bit of humour and I'd say, *"Well John that was one of your poorer efforts; four out of ten"* and it would stop him. I remember meeting him in the Dáil canteen one day, and he said; *"My God, you remind me of my mother, she could really take it."* His mother was a councillor and he was kind of giving me a compliment, even if he did still keep giving me all the flack!

When I was the Chair of the Development Aid Committee my two colleagues in that were Michael D. Higgins and Niall Andrews. It's a small thing, but when Bob Geldof's Live Aid record came out, there was VAT on it and I approached Garret about it. He suggested finding out how many records had been sold and what the VAT was, so I took myself round every record company in Dublin, discovered that it came to something like £200,000 and, as a result, Garret arranged for an extra £200,000 to go into the development aid budget. He was terrific.

John Bruton made me his Deputy Leader in 1993 and then in December '94 I became a minister literally overnight. Being involved in the Northern talks was a big highlight of my time as Minister for Justice and then the introduction of the Criminal Assets Bureau was enormous. It came about because of the murders of Veronica Guerin and Jerry McCabe. I had visited Veronica in hospital after the first time she was shot, I knew her family and I was heartbroken. I remember at her funeral a man outside the church shouted; *"What are you doing here? You're responsible for her death."* Mark Costigan stood between us and said, *"It's not her fault, this was a criminal who did this."* I could kind of understand the anger, but as a minister in any role, while you are responsible for making sure there's laws there and proper sentencing, you can't be held responsible if a criminal shoots somebody dead. We brought in the legislation in the shortest time ever, it was the Dáil and Senate working absolutely as it should. There were lots of other things, but the Criminal Assets Bureau has stood the test of time and I was really glad to have been part of the team that introduced the Criminal Assets Bureau.

The Alice Glenn Report

Vol.1 No.3   Box 1690 • Dublin 8   May 1986

A WOMAN VOTING FOR DIVORCE IS LIKE A TURKEY VOTING FOR CHRISTMAS

The report of the Oireachtas Joint Committee on Marriage Breakdown presented to the Dail in March 1985 contained the following passage: —

"Large scale unemployment, poor housing or inadequate financial resources can individually, or collectively place a marriage under strain and can exacerbate problems which may exist within marriage."

It is impossible to understand how the Government, armed as it was with this knowledge, could proceed to remove in the recent Budget all financial support for the families of the hard-pressed taxpayers.

You will recall the effects of this as outlined in my previous issue. Those in the 35% tax band gained 2p per week per child, the 48% band lost 23p per child per week and the 58% band lost 42p per child per week.

Prior to this, Equal Pay Legislation of 1974 made it a crime for an employer to give a married man extra pay to enable him to meet the extra costs of supporting a wife and children.

When you consider this irresponsible and unconstitutional treatment of the family, you will not be surprised to learn that many marriages are in trouble.

THE RIGHT TO REMARRY

The cure all for these ills as suggested by the Government is to introduce a **DIVORCE CULTURE** in our impoverished little nation, where the total revenue coming from the PAYE Sector i.e. £1900 million plus another £200 million is going to pay the annual interest on the National Debt of over £20,000 million. It will be difficult to convince the same long suffering taxpayers that they must now cough up a further £200 million, which is an approximate figure of the overall cost of supporting the Divorce Culture. This figure is based on the 70,000 persons (35,000 couples) argued by the divorce lobbies (and up to 100,000 persons mentioned by one of the leading pro-divorce dailies) who would immediately avail of legal divorce.

The figure is based on a pro-rata basis with the U.K. and includes the following services:

- Counselling Services
- Health Boards Grants and Services
- Extra Social Workers
- Home Advisory Personnel
- Extra Psychiatric and Psychological Services
- Medical Aid
- Free Legal Aid
- Halfway Homes as a Breathing Space
- The New Family Courts with all their Accoutrements, Paraphernalia, and Trappings.
- Ever Increasing Social Welfare Payments to Discarded Spouses and their Children.
- Numerous Other Factors that are hard to cost, e.g., Shattered Lives of Innocent Children who would have no say in the matter
- Child Abuse Including Sexual Abuse which often results from the Stranger who replaces the Natural Father (as experienced all too frequently in the U.K. and elsewhere)
- Increasing Numbers of Children requiring long-stay care in foster homes.

The Alice Glenn Report, 1986
Courtesy of Alan Kinsella, Irish Election Literature

1981–1992 Pushing Politics to Deliver Rights For Women

> *"I was a pioneer before the women's libbers even started."*

1981 TD
Alice Glenn

Teachta Dála for Dublin Central 1981-1982, 1982-1987

First female Chair of the Eastern Health Board

First woman to become a member of the Dublin Port and Docks Board

First woman to be elected to the Fine Gael National Executive

The deteriorating situation in Northern Ireland sparked Alice Glenn's initial motivation to get involved in politics. In a 1984 interview with Martin Lynch for the Young Fine Gael magazine *Futureline*, she recalled, *"It was 1969. I remember getting very angry watching Charles Haughey on television. It was the period of the Arms Crisis and I felt the next generation, including my ten year old son should not be used as cannon fodder."* She joined Fine Gael, but initially had no intention of ever becoming a public figure; *"I had always had a lot to say at meetings and enjoyed debates, but even on the very night of the 1973 election convention I had not even agreed to let my name go forward as a candidate".* Alice was persuaded to run in the constituency of Dublin North Central in the 1973 general election, but was unsuccessful. A second Dáil bid in Finglas in 1977 resulted in the same outcome, and she was eventually elected to the Dáil on her third attempt in 1981 to represent Dublin Central. She lost her seat in February 1982, and succeeded in winning it back in the November election that year, subsequently serving a five year term as a TD.

Alice Glenn's first experience of public life came in 1974 when she was elected to Dublin City Council. Housing and health quickly became her main areas of concern and between 1979 and 1981 she was twice Chairwoman of the Dublin City Housing Committee. In 1982 she became the first female Chair of the Eastern Health Board and her election literature that year describes her as, *"committed to seeking a better deal for the single woman in our society who has been overtaxed and neglected."* She was also strongly anti-communist and travelled with her husband to address a meeting of the World Anti-Communist League in Taiwan in 1984.

Her responsibilities on Dublin City Council led Alice into domains which had previously been male dominated, prompting her to assert in that same interview for *Futureline*, *"I was a pioneer before the women libbers even started."* Proud to have been the first woman Chairperson of the Housing

Committee, she also noted; *"Indeed I have a long list of firsts, the first woman on the Health Board, the first woman elected to the Fine Gael National Executive, first woman member of the Port and Docks Board."*

An understanding of poverty and the financial pressures often experienced by families were issues Alice Glenn revisited repeatedly in many of her Oireachtas contributions. Speaking on the Committee on Marital Breakdown Report in 1985 she observed that; *"Poverty, particularly when it affects children, causes domestic distress and discord with the risk of marital breakdown"*, and asked; *"How can parents be expected to fulfil their role in society if they are harassed daily by their inability to provide the basic food needed for proper nutrition, if meeting children's normal needs for shoes, clothing and school-books is a nightmare?"*

Above all else, she professed herself "a Catholic first and foremost" and the social conservatism she espoused was radically different to the views of many of her party colleagues at that time. Her unwavering adherence to those views meant that she was virulently anti-contraception, anti-divorce and anti-abortion and the positions she took frequently placed her in diametric opposition to the Party. She voted against the proposed Fine Gael-Labour wording on the 1983 amendment, opting instead to support the anti-abortion amendment to the constitution that year. She also opposed the Children's Care and Protection Bill in 1985 and famously wrote in *The Alice Glenn Report* of 1986 that, *"A woman voting for divorce is like a turkey voting for Christmas."*

In order to avoid expulsion she resigned from the Party, and in a 1987 article entitled, *Why Fine Gael Divorced Alice Glenn* she reflected that, *"My dilemma was how to remain on the national scene while being a member of a party I felt was being led by persons opposed to those values. I found myself in constant conflict with the Party leadership on fundamental Constitutional issues, affecting every family in the land."* In the election of 1987 she stood unsuccesfully as an independent candidate. Alice retired from political life when she lost her seat on Dublin City Council in 1991. She died following a long illness, one day short of her ninetieth birthday. The obituary in *The Irish Times* of 24th December, 2011 described her as *"a conviction politician whose patriotism was defined by her faith"*.

The eldest of ten children, Alice Glenn was born in Usher's Quay, Dublin in 1921. Her father was a motor mechanic and her mother came from a long-established family of Dublin coopers. She began her education at the Convent of Mercy in Stanhope Street, but the family's financial circumstances dictated that she had to leave school early to work at a tailoring firm. The conditions she found in her new place of employment so appalled her that she convinced her co-workers, most of whom were women, to join the Garment Workers' Union in a bid to improve their situation there. Later, she set up her own dressmaking business with her sister, and married Air Corps cadet Bill Glenn, who subsequently rose through the ranks to become Brigadier General. The couple had two sons.

> *"Poverty, particularly when it affects children, causes domestic distress and discord with the risk of marital breakdown."*

> The following excerpts from Alice Glenn's contribution on the bill to establish the Combat Poverty Agency provides a good example of many of her views on issues including poverty, housing, lone parents and families.

25 February 1986
Combat Poverty Agency Bill, 1985 (Seanad Second Stage)

At present we are seeing the feminisation of poverty. For example, in 1985 there were 900 applicants on Dublin Corporation housing lists. They were single parents, mainly women with children; there are very few men single parents. That constitutes almost three-quarters of the entire applications for housing in Dublin Corporation. Therein I see the feminisation of poverty. While we may give such people units of accommodation they are continuing to live in stressful circumstances. This is an area that must be examined for several reasons. Because there is no alternative to putting such people into one area of our housing stock we are now creating other problems where there is already massive poverty and deprivation. As I said yesterday at a meeting of the city council, we have had to demolish the entire inner city. Because of all of those in need being put into the inner city at one stage, the inner city became a no-go area vis-á-vis the forces of law and order. There was no alternative to taking them from that area and rebuilding. We are recreating that position by placing so many of these young women in that kind of situation, all together in one identifiable area. That is poverty at its worst, they being identified as a deprived section of the community, when their and their children's chances of ever taking a step up the rung of that ladder are remote. Those are the kinds of problems I would hope that Combat Poverty Agency would take account of.

... In yesterday's The Irish Times there was a headline to the effect that deserted wives and single parents were costing the State £60 million. I deal with the inner city. I know from my clinics, from my meetings with people, with the parents of some of these unfortunate unmarried mothers, that they do not thank us at all for what we are doing to them. I have been told that we are rendering it attractive for young girls to become unmarried mothers. I believe the reason for that is that young girls leaving school at 16 have no status at all in this State, they are non-persons, they do not qualify for anything. Many of them of whom I have knowledge come from homes in which there is already much unemployment. Therefore, having no source of income whatever, they are driven to desperation.

I visited a boy's school in the inner city just before Christmas. The principal of that school told me that he was aware of young men in that area being earmarked to become fathers of children of these young girls who were deliberately taking the decision they would have a child because it would set them up and give them a status. The problems for the State inherent in that concept, for the future of the family and stability of the State, are horrendous for those who take the trouble to analyse it. We are told there are 11,300 unmarried mothers and 9,000 deserted wives. The problem of the unmarried mother could be alleviated if we gave these young girls some kind of recognition some type of support, rather than leaving them penniless...

PROUD TO SERVE: The Voices of the Women of Cumann na nGaedheal and Fine Gael 1922-1992

On the campagn trail, 1981
Courtesy of Fine Gael

> "I'd advise any woman who's interested in getting involved in politics to do the research and weigh up exactly what's involved and how little family time you can expect to have."

1981 SENATOR
Deirdre Bolger

Senator 1981–1982, 1982–1983

Member Fine Gael National Executive

Chairperson of the South Eastern Health Board

Member of the first Committee of the Regions attached to the European Parliament

Rapporteur on the Good Friday Agreement at The Committee of The Regions

In 1978 Deirdre Bolger was co-opted onto Wexford County Council, retaining the seat at the local elections a year later. She was returned at every subsequent local election until her retirement from politics in 2004. She was twice elected to the Industrial and Commercial panel of the Seanad, in 1981 and 1982 respectively. Deirdre was also selected as a Fine Gael candidate in the 1984 European elections, but was unsuccessful on that occasion.

Over the years Deirdre held a number of local and regional positions within Fine Gael, including membership of the National Executive. As a member of Wexford County Council, her responsibilities included tenures as Chairperson of the South Eastern Health Board and the General Council of County Councils. She was also appointed to the first Committee of the Regions attached to the European Parliament for a four year term.

Deirdre grew up in a political household and trained as a nurse before moving to Gorey, Co. Wexford following her marriage to local Fine Gael Councillor David Bolger.

There were always politics in the house growing up, so it was nothing new to me when I got married. My father was a great friend of James Dillon, he was a very charismatic man and we used to see quite a bit of him. I was a nurse in my former life and I absolutely loved it, but I had to give up my job when I got married. People look at you now and they can't believe it, but that's the way it was. I could have eventually gone back to work, but with the recession jobs were minimal, particularly in a small community, and people would have been wondering "*why is she working?*" Then I got involved in politics.

My husband David was a County Councillor in Gorey, and as the Branch Secretary I did everything from making cups of tea to fundraising and organising socials. When David's only brother died, he had to take over the family business, so I was co-opted onto the council in his place. I ran in the next local elections and my first public function was representing the Gorey Town Commissioners at the Pope's visit to the Phoenix Park in 1979.

It's not easy for a woman. I had five boys, all steps of stairs and even though David was very good in supporting me and I had lots of help, I still had to plan and organise everything. I ran three Senate elections in the space of two years. It was a lot of driving on bad roads, you could be away for days and occasionally I'd bring the children with me, which wasn't ideal. It was very hard to get elected. At the end of the canvass you'd say, "well now, I got six votes today", and then you'd cut that in half, then cut it again. You just had to be smart about knowing how many votes you had, and even then you could be shafted at the last minute by somebody else. Politics is a tough game, and it's getting tougher.

The 1984 European elections were a major challenge for me. Mark Clinton and myself were the Fine Gael candidates. I had a great team of supporters. We would start our daily canvass early in the morning. Apart from organising the family at home, I was in the spotlight all the time between interviews on radio, TV and local papers. When I lost the election it was disappointing, but you have to take your beating and smile.

I got elected to the Seanad twice. It was very much a club and you had to earn your seniority. There weren't many women there at that time and because you were always thinking of the next election you couldn't afford to fall out with anybody. There was only one time I was really bold. Myself and Patsy Lawlor abstained during a motion in the Seanad to abolish capital punishment. Somebody said, "Could you not leave the chamber if you were going to abstain?" but it wasn't the same at all, and that did not go down well. We got our knuckles rapped and I'd say that was one of the reasons I didn't get elected to the Seanad again. You have to toe the line when you're in party politics.

The abortion issue was vicious, and it was very hot locally too. I wasn't in favour of abortion but there was one day SPUC came to the door and I had to ring the guards. That all died down, but then when you'd go canvassing you'd get a lot of that on the doorstep. I thought the debate around the recent referendum was very responsible. The usual hysteria around the subject was gone, so we've come a long way in a comparatively short space of time.

After all the public service I did in politics I never got a pension. I wasn't too bad in that my hubby always looked after me but there were men who lost out in those days and it was very serious for them. When I was on the Committee of the Regions there was no budget allocated for the first two years. You just got paid your airfare and your living expenses. It was a very long day, particularly if you had to speak or chair meetings. I was Rapporteur on the Good Friday Agreement in Brussels at the Committee of the Regions and that was a huge amount of work. I had to put it all together with very little secretarial help. I got a standing ovation at the end and that meant a lot to me.

> "At the end of the canvass you'd say, well now, I got six votes today, and then you'd cut that in half, then cut it again."

There were never more than two or three of us women in the Council. I think it's a pity because women bring a different aspect to everything. I think men have a huge advantage in politics. They get to cover a lot of their canvass and see a lot of people through sporting events and other associations, and if you're not involved in one of those, it was hard to make progress.

I hope the quota works but that in time it could be done away with. To be added to the ballot paper by HQ just because you're a woman doesn't give you a great start. I'd advise any woman who's interested in getting involved in politics to do the research and weigh up exactly what's involved and how little family time you can expect to have. Saying that, it's very rewarding too. Gorey is a very vibrant town now, there are lots of facilities in the area and I feel that I helped shaped the vision that facilitated its development. It was tough going but I made great friends and I enjoyed every bit of it.

WATERFORD SENATOR VOTES AGAINST
– DESPITE GARRET'S RECOMMENDATION

Contrary to the recommendation of party leader, Dr. Garret FitzGerald, Waterford Fine Gael Senator, Mrs. Katharine Bulbulia voted against the second stage of the Amendment of the Constitution Bill when it came before the Senate on Wednesday.

Her constituency colleague, Senator Michael Queally and the other 23 Fine Gael members abstained in accordance with a decision taken by the party's Senate group after the Bill had been passed by the Dail.

Senator Bulbulia supported a Labour Party motion calling for the rejection of the Fianna Fail wording of the amendment on the grounds that it was unclear, ambiguous and not the proper subject for a referendum proposal. The second stage, however, was passed by 18 votes to 15 and the committee stage will be taken next week.

Whether or not disciplinary action will be taken by the party against Senator Bulbulia is not clear. Some party members in Waterford are inclined to the opinion that while the matter will be discussed at the next meeting of the Fine Gael Parliamentary Party it is unlikely that a decision will be taken against her. Others, however, feel that she should have accepted her party leader's recommendation and that therefore action should be taken against her.

GRAVE DEFECTS IN F.F. WORDING

Contacted by a "Munster Express" reporter this morning, Mrs. Bulbulia said she was not yet aware whether or not she would be the subject of disciplinary action. She pointed out that the principle of conscience in the matter had been accepted by Fine Gael and that every Fine Gael Senator who spoke in the Senate debate pointed out the grave defects in the Fianna Fail wording of the amendment and the divisive character in the debate so far.

Senator Bulbulia explained that a maxim all her life had been that thought, speech and action should have uninterrupted flow and she saw no reason why she should depart from that on this occasion; in fact she found this a very particular occasion why she should adhere to that maxim.

SADDENED BY ABUSIVE CORRESPONDENCE

Having stressed that she was pro-life, Mrs. Bulbulia said she had been saddened by the abusive correspondence she had received from proponents of the amendment, extracts from which she read out during Wednesday's senate debate.

In the course of her Senate contribution, Senator Bulbulia said she had been impressed by the original movement for a Constitutional Amendment and had signed a letter supporting the proposal. On the face of it the amendment seemed to be an expression of our Christian values, but there had been little understanding in the early stages of the debate of the controversy the proposal would arouse. Few public representatives fully appreciated all the implications of the proposal initially, and some still appeared not to appreciate them. Her personal view was that some form of words might be useful in the Constitution but it was extremely doubtful if a satisfactory wording was possible.

Senator Bulbulia said she was deeply concerned that some 3,000 Irish women, and possibly twice that number, went to England each year for abortions. The implication was that as many as 50,000 women living in Ireland today had had abortions. She would have expected all the concern shown for the amendment to have led to a limate of concern and compassion for these women and those likely to follow them. This was not the case.

LEGAL IMPLICATIONS

Senator Bulbulia said she agreed with all Senator Mary Robinson had said on the legal implications. Many of the pro-amendment activists were motivated by genuine concern, but the unpleasant spectre of some of the most reactionary groups in society was at the helm of the campaign.

She had noted that one of the leaders of SPUC had gone on the record as opposing a society set up to concern itself with the sexuality of disabled people. This pointed to the sick minds at work in the campaign.

She criticised what she called the vilification of a leading and respected clergyman, Dean Griffin, during the Dail debate. After she had issued a statement apologising for this unwarranted attack she had received a number of sectarian letters couched in obscene language, presumably from a member of the moral majority. She mentioned this, she said, to illustrate the can of worms that was about to be opened.

Ecumenism and pluralism were vital areas if there was to be unity by consent which was the policy of all parties in the House, she said. The amendment was at the very heart of the degate about pluralism.

She said the Attorney-General had drawn attention to the Fianna Fail wording and said that it could probably lead to a situation where operations currently carried out to save the life of the mother might be stopped. As far as the Taoiseach was concerned this led to him repudiating this wording and by doing this he ran a great political risk, but he and the Government had integrity.

THREATENED ECUMENISM

She said the debate over the amendment had threatened ecumenism.

Senator Bulbulia said she believed in the constitutional crusade and in building a united Ireland.

The issue, she said, should never have been made a party political controversy and those politicians who had made it so had shamed themselves and the country. She appealed to the Taoiseach and to the leaders of the other political parties in the Oireachtas to reconsider their position. The matter was not urgent. There was time for reconsideration.

Senator Bulbulia said she supported the Labour Party amendment, and would not be abstaining on the vote as her party leader had recommended. she had listed carefully to Professor Dooge's explanation of the Fine Gael policy of abstention and it seemed to her that Fine Gael had become caught up in the niceties and intricacies of political and parliamentary strategy. The public would not comprehend that. The vote in the Senate would probably show a majority of about 18 to 15 for the Fianna Fail wording but that would be a distortion of the actual views of the House.

Munster Express, 1983
Courtesy of Irish Newspaper Archive

1981–1992 Pushing Politics to Deliver Rights For Women

"I pushed at boundaries that eventually other people felt were worth pushing at."

1981 SENATOR
Katharine Bulbulia

Senator 1981–1989

First woman elected to Waterford County Council

Founder member WPA Waterford branch

Programme Manager to Tánaiste Mary Harney 1997–2006

Katharine Bulbulia grew up in Sandymount in Dublin and moved to Waterford with her husband Abdul and two small children in 1973. Quickly immersing herself in social issues, she joined the Women's Political Association and the local branch of Fine Gael, before winning a seat in the local elections of 1979. Unsuccessful in three general election campaigns for Fine Gael, she ran for the Senate in 1981 and was subsequently elected four times in succession, narrowly missing out on her fifth attempt in 1989.

Following a series of local internecine party battles, Katharine resigned her council seat and devoted her energies to promoting the city through the auspices of Waterford Chamber of Commerce. She later joined the Progressive Democrats and ran unsuccessfully as a candidate in the 1997 general election. Katharine was Programme Manager to Tánaiste Mary Harney from 1997 to 2006, and more recently worked with The Association of European Parliamentarians with Africa (AWEPA) to provide capacity building in the newly emerging Southern African democracies.

I was fascinated by public life and particularly fascinated by Garret Fitzgerald. Here was a fresh voice talking about a pluralist society and a constitutional crusade, and he spoke to something within me that I cared deeply about. In 1973 industry was beginning to get underway in Waterford, so I helped found a group of women to welcome newly arrived people to the city. Then I heard about the Women's Political Association (WPA). I had known Gemma Hussey when I was a student in UCD, so I went to some meetings, then went back to my group to discuss setting up a Waterford WPA. There had never been a woman elected to Waterford County Council, there was no woman in Waterford City Council, and no female TD or female senator. If the decisions being made were going to affect the whole of society why were we absent? I invited Gemma,

Hilary Pratt, Mavis Arnold and various others to speak, and on a snowy day in January we filled the ballroom of the Tower Hotel.

Meanwhile I joined Fine Gael. I took it upon myself to knock on the door of Party headquarters in Waterford and what I found inside was not a party of Garret Fitzgerald, it was a deeply conservative grouping which dwelt on past glories. They used to talk about the Redmonds and Parnell, and I would talk about social issues and a constitutional crusade. The composition of the Fine Gael Party in Waterford at the time was more than two thirds men, of a certain age, absolutely loyal to the sitting TD Eddie Collins. However there were a few forward thinking people with whom I bonded.

When the 1979 local elections loomed I began to look for a woman candidate and somebody suggested that I put myself forward. I'd never participated in an election but I had a powerful network, so I decided to give it a go. I headed the poll in the Tramore electoral area with twice as many votes as Eddie Collins. I was being lionised by Peter Prendergast, Garret Fitzgerald and everybody in Dublin, not by the party locally, I hasten to add, they couldn't stand my guts. Eddie Collins immediately saw me as a threat. Austin Deasy had been very supportive of me because he wanted to have the whole pie to himself, and I was going to be, in hindsight I see it all now, a very useful pawn in a game of party politics.

Off I went to the meetings in Waterford County Council and I was like a rare bird. The lads would move motions congratulating this team and that team on winning the county finals, so I did my homework and camogie began to get a mention too. Then they all went across the road for a jar and I went home. I learned that you were basically ineffectual, and that who actually ran the Council was the City and County Managers and the staff, but you could do some advocacy and I was quite good at that.

My vision of politics then was that you were a bit like a social worker. I remember one woman living in a local authority estate who had been bashed up by her husband, and going to the then County Manager and pleading that we had to get a separate house for this woman and her children or something awful was going to happen. He sat me down and said, "We cannot in our policy and in our decision-making do anything to separate a family." My agenda was to do with social reform, the improvement of the status of women and giving women a chance, so I joined with others and we founded Oasis, a refuge for women in Waterford city.

In 1981 it was put to me that I might run for the Senate, so I began this odyssey of a journey, and when I think that it hasn't been reformed today I just despair. It is the weirdest, most punishing campaign and I did it three times within eighteen months. I used to get elected handsomely enough and I liked the Senate debating chamber. I was interested in development cooperation and economics, so they made me Finance Spokesperson for Fine Gael in the Seanad. I learned an awful lot and I'm very grateful to all the people who helped and encouraged me there.

> "My agenda was to do with social reform, the improvement of the status of women and giving women a chance."

I was absolutely convinced that the Eighth Amendment was wrong, and would lead to trouble. Peter Sutherland, the then Attorney General, had spoken to me and I saw that Garret had been caught in a bind, so I broke the whip and voted with the Labour Party against it. I remember shaking in my shoes and saying to Maurice Manning, "I'll be out on my ear". He said, "Garret isn't mad with you, he almost expected that you'd do that". Garret loved women and there was nobody more encouraging. I still have a book where he wrote in the flyleaf, "Don't let the men get you down". In Waterford I was the only one who was a social democrat within Fine Gael, so I campaigned in favour of divorce. That didn't make life easy, but I absolutely believed in the rightness of what I was about. I didn't think about whether you'd pay an electoral price. It wasn't my bread and butter so that gave me a certain freedom, and even if it had been, I probably would have done the same.

I'd had all this rowing with Fine Gael locally and the National Executive of the Party took it on and expelled a councillor, because at one stage when I was in the City Council the Party, apart from one person, ganged up against me with Fianna Fáil to block me from committee membership. It was ugly and nasty and deeply stressful. My husband is of Indian origin, he came here when he was young and studied medicine. This was not multiracial Ireland and I remember somebody saying disparagingly; "Banotti and fecking Bulbulia, the Fine Gael Party is beginning to sound like an Italian football team."

In general elections I was always the candidate that John Healy called "the hind tit merchant" who shored up the seat. When I decided I wasn't going to do that again, Eddie Collins lost the seat and since then there hasn't been a Fine Gael TD in Waterford City. Austin Deasy was very good to me but once Eddie Collins was off the scene he basically told me I was on my own. Dessie O'Malley asked me to run for the PDs in 1987 and I said no because I'd given loyalty to Garret Fitzgerald. After I failed to get elected to the Senate in 1989, I stayed on the City Council for a while, but they were still at it. I found it dissipating of my energy and whatever bit of talent I had, so I left. I went to work with the Chamber of Commerce as its first Executive Director. Then Mary Harney asked me to run for the PDs. I had a go at that, but it was a disastrous campaign for the PDs.

I was very idealistic and all I could think of was helping people and making things happen as best I could. That was my thing, pushing out the boat, inviting people to think beyond what we were being fed, and getting an idea to take root and bear fruit. I pushed at boundaries that eventually other people felt were worth pushing at. For me it is an absolute that we need more women in politics and I am very much in favour of quotas, but I hope they will only last for a certain period of time until we reach a critical mass. The final chapter of my political career as Programme Manager was personally very satisfying in participating in politics at the highest level.

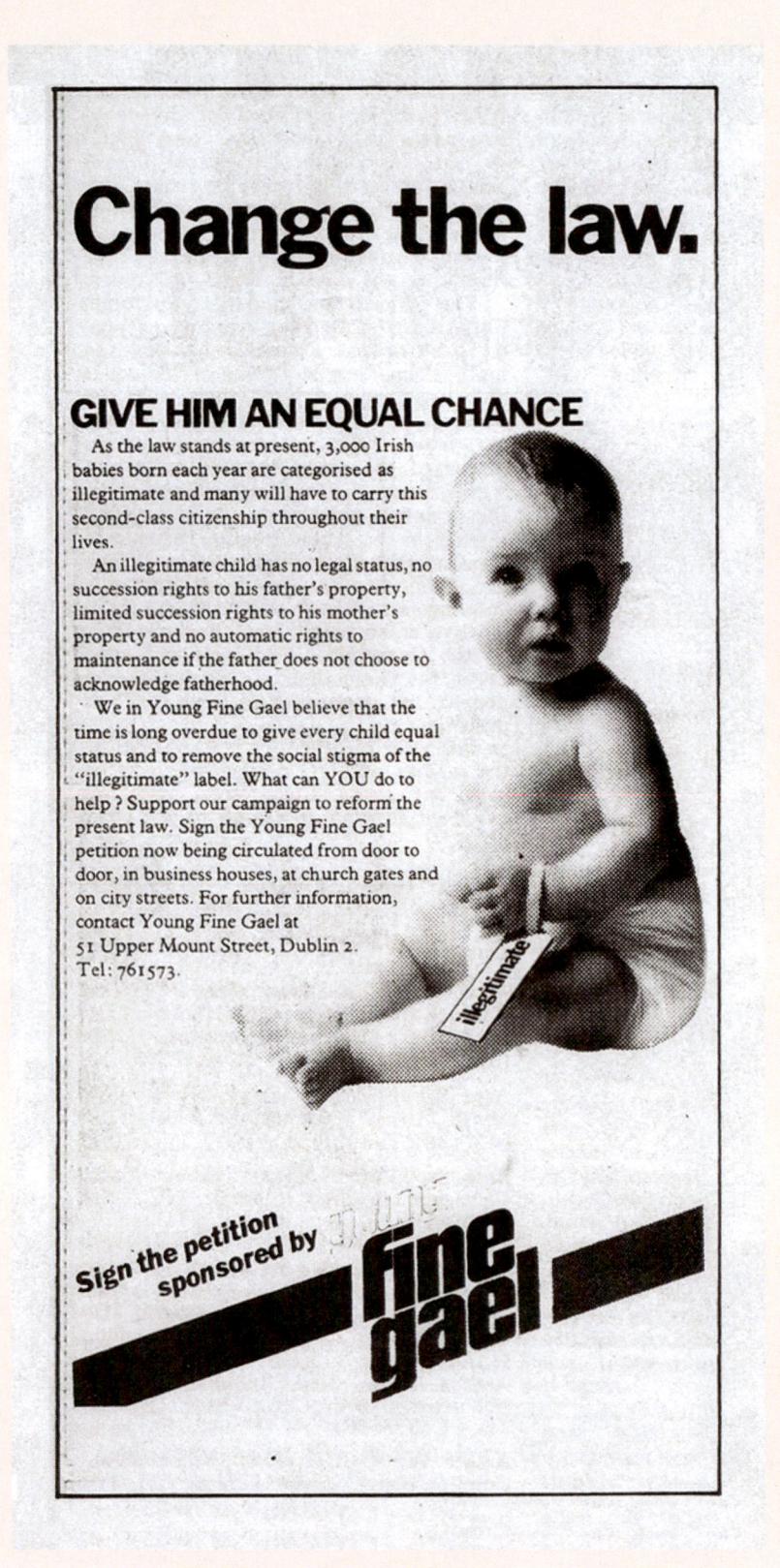

PROUD TO SERVE: The Voices of the Women of Cumann na nGaedheal and Fine Gael 1922-1992

Change the law.

GIVE HIM AN EQUAL CHANCE

As the law stands at present, 3,000 Irish babies born each year are categorised as illegitimate and many will have to carry this second-class citizenship throughout their lives.

An illegitimate child has no legal status, no succession rights to his father's property, limited succession rights to his mother's property and no automatic rights to maintenance if the father does not choose to acknowledge fatherhood.

We in Young Fine Gael believe that the time is long overdue to give every child equal status and to remove the social stigma of the "illegitimate" label. What can YOU do to help? Support our campaign to reform the present law. Sign the Young Fine Gael petition now being circulated from door to door, in business houses, at church gates and on city streets. For further information, contact Young Fine Gael at 51 Upper Mount Street, Dublin 2. Tel: 761573.

Sign the petition sponsored by **fine gael**

Ephemera on changing the law on illegitimacy, 1980
Courtesy of Alan Kinsella, Irish Election Literature

1981–1992 Pushing Politics to Deliver Rights For Women

> "It was a fascinating Senate and it was a privilege to be there."

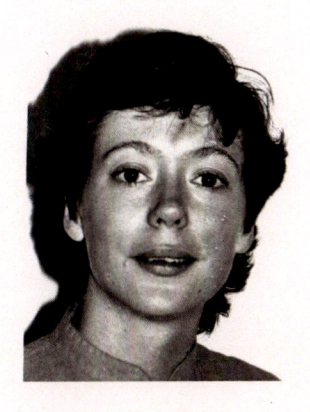

1981 SENATOR
Miriam Kearney

Senator 1981–1982

First female Assistant General Secretary of Fine Gael

Chair of the Young Fine Gael International Committee

Deputy General Secretary of the European Union of Young Christian Democrats

When Taoiseach Garret Fitzgerald named Miriam Kearney as one of his eleven Seanad nominees in 1981, the appointment of the twenty-two year old political activist reflected the Fine Gael leader's commitment to fostering the inclusion of more women and younger people in politics.

The electoral turbulence that characterised Irish politics in the early 1980s meant that the Seanad to which Miriam was appointed lasted only six months. While her tenure in parliamentary politics was short-lived, her own political involvement proved much more enduring.

Miriam had been a member of Young Fine Gael prior to her appointment having served as Chair of its International Committee and as Deputy General Secretary of the European Union of Young Christian Democrats. She was involved in a number of Young Fine Gael initiatives, including the campaign to abolish the status of illegitimacy. She worked in Party headquarters from 1981 to 1987, initially as National Youth Officer and subsequently as Assistant General Secretary. She continues to be an active volunteer for the Party.

The main reason I got involved in politics was because I was inspired to do so by Garret Fitzgerald. I liked his commitment to the ideals of the Just Society policy and his inclusive approach to Unionism in Northern Ireland. As a country we were moving out from the closed Ireland of the 1930s, '40s and '50s, and I was impressed by his vision of an open, progressive, modern Ireland committed to Europe. When he became leader, he undertook fairly radical change in the organisation of the Party, Young Fine Gael was established and it was quite an exciting time to be involved. I joined in university and I've been a member ever since.

Garret was probably a feminist well before many of his male contemporaries would have understood that term. He also appointed people to senior roles within the Party who were themselves committed to encouraging women, and Dan Egan who ran Young Fine Gael would have been a big mentor to me. Many of those who came into the Dáil and Seanad in 1981 were newly recruited into the Party, and prior to that they would have been involved in the women's movement, education or some other aspect of public life. I had been a very active member of Young Fine Gael in a variety of different capacities, so as a woman and a young person, my appointment covered two key groups that the Party was working to include at the time.

In that particular Senate, Garret also appointed Jim Dooge and made him Minister for Foreign Affairs, Jim was an amazing man who gave me great support and encouragement, as did another significant mentor and fellow Taoiseach's nominee Sean O'Leary. I remember going in and thinking "Wow! Here I am with people like Mary Robinson and Catherine McGuinness." Gemma Hussey was leader and we were still talking about the abolition of capital punishment. It was a fascinating Senate and it was a privilege to be there. I also attended parliamentary party meetings, and it was amazing to have a front row seat in the legislative process.

At the same time I was also National Youth Officer, and I figured within a short time of getting involved in parliamentary politics that I was probably more suited to a backroom role. After the fall of that government in 1982, I became Assistant General Secretary and went on to work within the senior Party until 1987. It was a very intense but rewarding time.

The Young Fine Gael campaign to abolish the status of illegitimacy was one of its most significant campaigns. Other organisations were also campaigning hard on the issue, but we were the youth wing of an established party taking this on, pushing to get it included in manifestos, and we successfully campaigned to convince members of the senior Party to adopt it as policy.

We got a lot of opposition too. In many cases the arguments ultimately came down to arguments about property and they were the same kind of arguments that later featured in the divorce referendum. The change in the law in that area was an important achievement, and it opened a debate around all kinds of questions about the role of women and children and the way we treated women and children, not just single mothers but also married women. The issues we dealt with then continued to echo right up to the recent referendum to repeal the 8th Amendment.

The referendum in 1983 was a very unfortunate step backwards. I've a recollection of very intense discussions between people with strong opinions and convictions on both sides of the issue, while others were trying to build some kind of consensus around what was best for the country. Some of the stuff that was around in that referendum was very distasteful, everything from foetuses in jars and really vile letters being sent into Party headquarters. We had a good supportive staff network, and I don't think it was ever as vicious as the kind of things that political activists and politicians have to put up with nowadays from social media.

> "Having people within the senior ranks of party staff actively encouraging women is crucial."

Young Fine Gael meeting at HQ, 1980s

It would be wrong to look back on that period and think it was dominated by the social debates. Dealing with the economic problems and Northern Ireland were the two biggest challenges faced by that government. We were dealing with the fallout from the '77 manifesto which had significantly damaged the tax base, and at the same time a lot of manufacturing business was closing down. The nature of the political challenges may differ from generation to generation but health, education, social welfare and tax, are always going to be the key issues that politicians and governments have to deal with.

The decision to provide a financial penalty if parties did not run a certain percentage of women has been significant in changing the landscape in terms of women getting involved in politics. For a lot of men, involvement in politics is almost part of their social life. That can be the case for many women too, but a significant number still have a disproportionate share of the domestic and caring duties in family life and they have to be more careful with their time. A political system that demands a lot of hanging around and night-time meetings is not a priority for them. The fact that parties now have targets for general elections means that they have to go out and proactively look at how they encourage and recruit potential women candidates.

Having people within the senior ranks of Party staff actively encouraging women is crucial. I also think that older women have a huge amount to contribute, so parties could encourage the next generation of female candidates by going out and seeking to involve those who are already active in their community or campaigning on issues. In my experience women are much more interested in policy than they are in the mechanics of political organisations. A lot of what ends up in manifestos and Party policy is written by people working for parties in a voluntary capacity with an expertise in certain areas, so it's also very important that there are female voices in the backroom advisory and policy-making roles.

Parties are also looking at new ways to recruit members, retain and engage with members, and the old model of branches and meetings is evolving.

As parties look to engage activists and members in a different way, I think that the change in how parties manage themselves will suit women better.

"For too long well-heeled articulate men have been legislating for us. It's about time we stood up and were counted."

1981 SENATOR
Patsy Lawlor

Senator 1981–1983

First female Chair Kildare County Council

Chair of the General Council of County Councils

President Irish Countrywomen's Association (ICA) 1976–1979

Founder of the Kill Guild of the Irish Countrywomen's Association (ICA)

In 1961 Patsy Lawlor founded the Kill Guild of the Irish Countrywomen's Association (ICA). She went on to serve a three year term as the organisation's National President from 1976 to 1979 and her presidency was characterised by a progressive attitude to the role of women in society. She advanced the view that the ICA *"would have to face up to issues such as contraception"* and supported the increased representation of women in politics. In one media interview during this period she urged more women to get involved in political life noting that, *"Local Government elections are coming up in the next few years and women must get themselves involved in the decision making areas."*

During the course of a speech on *The ICA and a Changing Society* at the organisation's Winter Council meeting in February 1978, Patsy took the opportunity to address controversial remarks made by the then Minister for Finance George Colley. He had referred to the views of the Married Persons Tax Reform Association as those of *"well-heeled, articulate women"*, provoking the ire of those who were aware that the organisation represented many women including widows with virtually no income. To the enthusiastic applause of her colleagues she used the Minister's own words to make the following observations, which were subsequently reported in *The Irish Times* under the headline; *"Colley Attacked by ICA President";*

"For too long well-heeled articulate men have been legislating for us. It's about time we stood up and were counted. Mr Colley like many more has decided to drive a wedge between women. This has kept small farmers apart from big farmers, urban apart from rural, North apart from South. United we stand divided we fall. Mr Colley was referring to 15% of the total workforce – which is the percentage of the workforce represented by married women. It is the right of every man and woman (and child) who wishes to work. I disagree with what Mr Colley says and may I say that this is not the last he will be hearing from 26,000 well-heeled articulate women."

Councillor Patsy Lawlor
Courtesy of Marjorie Moore

Parallel to her involvement in the ICA and activities in her native county, Patsy Lawlor joined Fine Gael. 1974 saw her election to Kildare County Council, where she became its first woman Chair and was also the first female Chairperson of Kildare Vocational Education Committee (VEC). A member of Naas UDC, Patsy was Chair of the General Council of County Councils and was also appointed to the Arts Council in 1975. Having unsuccessfully sought a nomination on the Fine Gael Party ticket in 1977, she was selected four years later to contest the general election in the constituency of Kildare. Her 1981 election platform emphasised the particular needs of young people and school leavers and sought improvements in social welfare and the health services. On that occasion she lost out to Alan Dukes by less than fifty votes, and later reflected; *"It was my biggest disappointment when I was eliminated... My work record is good. I do what is asked of me by my constituents."*

Patsy continued to promote equal rights for women and during a debate at the 1981 Fine Gael Ard Fheis said that; *"An amendment should be made to the Family Home Protection Act 1976 to ensure joint ownership between husband and wife. It would ensure a further safety for the wife and children."* She secured a seat in Seanad Éireann in 1981 where she exercised the right of "conscientious dissent" and abstained on the vote on hanging during the second stage of the Criminal Justice Bill.

A businesswoman as well as a politician Patsy Lawlor (née Broughal) was born in March 1933, and educated at Kill National School and St Mary's Secondary School in Naas. She trained and worked as a nurse before marrying Kildare farmer Tony Lawlor, and in common with many other working women of her generation, had to give up her job on marriage. Patsy subsequently forged a new career managing a Bed and Breakfast business from the family farmhouse and, in addition to raising four children, also took over the running of the family pub after the death of her brother.

Patsy Lawlor left Fine Gael in 1985 and later unsuccessfully contested the 1992 election as an independent. She remained an Independent Councillor until her death on 19th December, 1997, and was succeeded on the Council by her son Anthony. In the many expressions of sympathy in the Oireachtas following her death, her former colleagues extolled her enormous energy, dedication and vitality, her gregarious nature and extraordinary knowledge of the people and politics of County Kildare.

> "It is only when we understand the meaning of Decision-Making and Co-Partnership together with Co-Responsibilities in the management of our own homes and businesses can progress for women begin."

Patsy Lawlor delivered the following speech as President of the Irish Countrywomen's Association at the organisation's Summer Council meeting in Portlaoise in July 1976.

The Three Dimensional Role of Women

This role well recognised elsewhere has not yet come to the surface in this country. Today I am taking the woman in the Farm Family as a practical illustration.

1. **Home Manager or Co-Manager** - Involves decisions and skills. This role is basic to all home situations. Timothy J. Twomey, Agricultural Advisor for Co. Laois, has carried out a study and survey of the "Involvement of Farmwives in Farm, Farm-Home & Family Decisions and Tasks." He has found that the majority of the home decisions and the Farm Home Tasks are performed by the farmwife with the exception of those which require a high level of mechanical skill.

2. **Socio/Emotional Role - Wife/Mother** - Family Decisions - Again basic to all family situations. In general it can be stated that the wife is more involved than the husband in family decision issues.

3. **Economic or Production Role in The Enterprise** - Here the Enterprise is the Farm with its particular demands and satisfactions. The role of worker, co-worker, partner or administrator is common to most family situations especially at the development stage. Has this role been over played in the family business in general and the farm family in particular? Studies in other European countries indicate 500 - 1500 hours per annum worked by women on the Farm Enterprise, particularly those enterprises based on dairying or small livestock. Studies here indicate that a similar situation exists. We as women do not need studies to indicate this situation, as we know it, because this triple role is part of our everyday lives. We do however, need organised studies to show and to prove to society at large, the unrecognised, unacknowledged subsidy to the Family provided by the hidden day-to-day work of its women.

We should be aware of our Decision Making role within all three, be careful of conflict, allowing for traditional attitudes. Understandings of one by another of the problems as well as the advantages. New developments should be anticipated and tackled before tensions and antagonisms develop. It is only when we understand the meaning of Decision-Making and Co-Partnership together with Co-Responsibilities in the management of our own homes and businesses can progress for women begin. Then we can claim to be adequately fitted to take part in the Co-Partnership of the Management of our Communities and of our Nation.

PROUD TO SERVE: The Voices of the Women of Cumann na nGaedheal and Fine Gael 1922-1992

Monica Barnes outside the Dáil
Courtesy of Sarah Barnes

1981–1992 Pushing Politics to Deliver Rights For Women

"Every step is hard work, but when women get into power they transform not just politics, but society."

1982 SENATOR and TD
Monica Barnes

Senator 1982

Teachta Dála for Dun Laoghaire 1982–1992; 1997–2002

Member of the Council of State 1991–1995

Member of the Women's Rights Committee 1982–1992

Co-founder of the Council for the Status of Women (CSW)

Founder of Women Elect

A life-long champion of women's rights, Monica Barnes (née MacDermott) was born in February 1936 and spent her formative years in Kingscourt, Co. Cavan, where her father, a committed trade unionist, worked at the local Gypsum Industries factory. The promising young student won a scholarship to attend St Louis Convent in Carrickmacross, and in later life stoically recalled the moment that her mind went blank while doing her Leaving Certificate maths exam. The subject was a requirement for entry to university, and with the option of studying for a degree closed off to her, Monica completed a short course in journalism and business studies, then emigrated to London. During her time in the city she undertook a number of jobs, including a stint as a secretary in the London Stock Exchange at a time when women were not allowed work on the floor of that particular institution.

On her return to Ireland Monica married Robert (Bob) Barnes and the couple had three children. She continued to work for the Dublin-based printers involved in producing the Dáil Reports following her marriage, but had to leave her job when she was five months pregnant. Experiencing postnatal depression, Monica's request for assistance was met by an unsupportive doctor dispensing a brusque instruction; "Pull yourself together Woman". Monica quickly realised that there was no help available and immediately set about organising a support group for women with postnatal depression. That initiative set her on the path that would define her political career, and she became increasingly interested in equality and women's rights.

In 1973 Monica was instrumental in co-founding the Council for the Status of Women (CSW), and also got involved in the Women's Political Association (WPA). When that organisation split in 1974, Monica established Women Elect, a support organisation for political women across all party lines. She began contacting those women who had taken the first step towards national politics by getting elected to their local Councils, and regarded the connections and networks forged during this period as invaluable in sowing the seeds for future cross-party collaboration amongst women in the Dáil.

During that period Monica was also involved in Fine Gael, sharing the progressive liberal political beliefs espoused by the Fitzgerald wing of the Party. She was nominated as a Fine Gael candidate to contest the European Parliament elections for the constituency of Leinster in 1979, and that campaign provided an early glimpse into her clear-sighted ability to get to the heart of an issue. When it was mooted that the campaign being mounted by the Women's Political Association was discriminating against men, she observed, *"In other words the 96% are accusing the 4% of discrimination for attempting to improve their relative position"*. That election and two further bids for a Dáil seat in 1981 and February 1982 proved unsuccessful, but in 1982 Monica was elected to Seanad Éireann. That November she was returned as a Fine Gael TD for the constituency of Dun Laoghaire, where she successfully held her seat for the next ten years.

Throughout her time in politics Monica proved a consistent and diligent advocate for those on the margins of Irish society. She worked tirelessly to progress a number of important issues including the legalisation of contraception, divorce, homosexuality and abortion at a time when these issues were conventionally regarded as beyond the pale in Ireland. Her opposition to the proposed wording of the 1983 abortion referendum resulted in her breaking the Party whip in the Dáil and in 1998 she wrote to the Ancient Order of Hibernians to protest at their exclusion of gay and lesbian groups from marching in the St Patrick's Day parade. In the decade between 1982 and 1992 she was a member of the cross-party Women's Rights Committee in the Dáil, which was chaired by herself and Máire Geoghegan-Quinn.

Appointed by President Mary Robinson as a Member of the Council of State from 1991 - 1995, Monica again campaigned unsuccessfully for a seat in the European Parliament in 1994. After a gap of five years she returned to the Dáil in 1997 and retired from parliamentary politics at the general election of 2002. In reviewing her career at that time, some commentators expressed surprise that she had never been appointed to ministerial office, but as the prolific campaigner was often reminded; *"The pioneers take the arrows, the settlers take the land."* She continued to remain politically active and at the time of her sudden death in May 2018 was preparing to take an active role in the Campaign to Repeal the Eighth Amendment. In the midst of the many tributes paid to Monica Barnes following her passing, the accolade most frequently used to describe her life and work was "Trailblazer".

> *"I still think politics is the most powerful career and there is still so much to do. Women can't afford to stay outside."*

Shortly before her unexpected death in May 2018, Monica Barnes recorded an interview as part of a college dissertation being completed by her granddaughter Ailbhe Hennessy, during the course of which she shared some thoughts on women's participation in politics. We are indebted to Ailbhe and to Monica's daughter Sarah for their generosity in sharing excerpts from that section of the recording, an edited version of which is reproduced below.

One of the great debates in the Women's Movement from the 1970s onwards was whether women should reject male power and institutions, or enter them in order to improve the status of women and effect changes in policy and legislation. I still think politics is the most powerful career and there is still so much to do. Women can't afford to stay outside.

The main obstacles to women going into politics are institutional barriers, but these exist for women not just in politics, but also in the City, tech firms, etc. This treatment is not new. Think of the suffragettes. They were mostly women who were educated and of high status. They suffered the most unbelievable treatment, forced feeding, physical abuse and huge derision. During World War One they decided to hold an amnesty in respect of their demands to help with the war effort and afterwards Britain knew that it couldn't suppress their demands for much longer.

I think that women have a different approach and can influence men. It is about giving them a vision and allowing them to take hold of it as well. Men will work seven days a week often doing work to make themselves more important. Women stand back and think, "*Is this it – do I have to sacrifice everything for this? I have one life.*" They often find these worlds too male dominated, arid, unrewarding, counter to family and to community. Not only do they believe that their commitment to their children or family is huge, but also to other interests outside of work and home.

In research undertaken by Dr Frances Gardiner, one Canadian woman parliamentarian said, "*Women don't care about losing face, because they never had face to lose to begin with. Men will start a war rather than lose face*"; while another said; "*Men work and think towards the next election, women work and think towards their grandchildren.*" Think of the so-called "Blair Babes" who were elected in the Labour Party in the United Kingdom – how many of them dropped out of public life afterwards?

After I left the WPA I realised that there were many women around Ireland who had reached the first step in trying to get elected to the Dáil, mostly they had succeeded in getting elected to a County Council. I set up Women Elect (WE) and wrote to each of these women and asked them if they would like to join.

The organisation crossed party lines, and women from all the main political parties joined. The organisation was very successful, and between the 1981 and 1982 elections fourteen of the women in Women Elect got elected to the Dáil. We proved to be a very powerful small caucus as we all knew one another from our time in Women Elect, and continued to work across party lines on issues that primarily affected women. We were aware that this unity was regarded with huge suspicion from male politicians.

Between 1982 - 87 and 1987 - 92 the Women's Rights Committee sat and was chaired by myself and by Máire Geoghegan-Quinn. One of the things I am most proud of is that every decision reached by the Committee was discussed and decisions were reached by consensus and never once did a vote have to be held. I believe that Angela Merkel is so successful because she operates outside party lines and because she has a view of working with people towards the national good, not just in Germany, but in Europe. This is very important now when Europe is splintering.

Things are gradually changing. Compared with my time and trying to get through the Conventions it is easier for women to get through them today and easier for them to run. I am thrilled that the women politicians have set up a "Women's Caucus" and have linked up with other women's caucuses in other countries. Every step is hard work, but when women get into power they transform not just politics, but society.

1981–1992 Pushing Politics to Deliver Rights For Women

FINE GAEL WOMEN FOR DIVORCE . . . Pictured at yesterday's Press Conference are (from left) Madeline Taylor-Quinn TD, Mary Flaherty TD, Nora Owen TD, and Gemma Hussey, Minister for Social Welfare.

Irish Press, 1986
Courtesy of Irish Newspaper Archive

> "I do believe that role models are important, and I hope that in a few short years, there won't be a need for quotas."

1982 TD, SENATOR and MEP
Avril Doyle

Teachta Dála for Wexford 1982–1987, 1987–1989 1992–1997

First female TD for the Wexford Constituency

Minister of State for the Department of the Environment (with special responsibility for Environmental protection), and the Department of Finance with responsibility for the Office of Public Works (OPW)

Member of the European Parliament 1999 - 2009

Rapporteur for the European Parliament on the Emissions Trading Directive

Leader of the Irish Delegation in the European People's Party 1999–2009

First woman to be elected Mayor of Wexford

In 1974 Avril Doyle took the first step in a political career that would see her serving thirty-five years as a public representative, when she was elected to Wexford County Council and Wexford Corporation. In 1976 she became the first woman to be elected Mayor of Wexford. When Avril was elected to Dáil Éireann in November 1982, she was the first woman to be elected a TD for the Wexford Constituency. She was appointed Minister of State by Taoiseach Garret Fitzgerald in her first term. Having retained her seat in 1987, she lost out to her Fine Gael colleague Michael D'Arcy in the 1989 general election but was subsequently elected to Seanad Éireann on the Agricultural Panel. She was re-elected to Dáil Éireann in 1992, but again lost her Dáil seat to her party colleague at the 1997 general election followed by re-election to the Seanad.

Avril served as a Minister of State in the Fine Gael-Labour Party coalition governments of 1982 – 87 and 1994 – 97. She later served two terms as a Member of the European Parliament, where she was leader of the Irish Delegation in the group of the European People's Party (EPP) for ten years. One of only three female members of Fine Gael to have served in the Dáil, the Seanad and the European Parliament, Avril retired as a member of the European Parliament in 2009. Prior to entering politics, she co-founded The Chic shop in Wexford town and also spent time as a substitute teacher in maths and science. She is a former president of the Equestrian Federation of Ireland and is currently a public affairs adviser and Associate Member of the British Veterinary Association.

There was never a moment when I made a decision "to go into politics". I did join the John Marcus O'Sullivan branch at UCD, mainly because my boyfriend at the time was a member! As a youngster I was never overly politicised, even though my father was Cathaoirleach of the Borough of Dun Laoghaire a number of times and a one-term Senator from 1969 - 73. My grandfather, Paddy Belton senior, had an interesting and chequered history as a TD, but my mother had little interest, so it was rarely discussed at home.

In 1971 I married and moved to Wexford. I had a small baby and was about to have a second when the local Party elders approached me ahead of the 1974 local elections. Would I stand? I laughed at them and said, "You are joking?!" As at that stage the election wasn't for another six months and probably without having a very clear idea of what I was walking into, I let my name go forward. I got elected to both the Corporation and the County Council (at odds of 200/1), and in June 1976 I became Mayor of Wexford. I was, by now, seriously committed. Local government is very compatible with a young family, you're living in your community, and I spent nearly twenty years as a member of Wexford County Council.

The Party asked me several times to stand for the Dáil, but because I'd had a third baby and the children were still very young, I declined. When I finally ran for the first time in 1982, I thought my chances of election were slim as we had two incumbent Fine Gael TDs, but against the odds we took three seats out of five. I was delighted to be made a Minister of State for the Department of the Environment, and the Department of Finance with responsibility for the Office of Public Works (OPW), in my first term in the Dáil. There had been no female minister in the Department of the Environment before I was appointed so they did up an office for me, with a room for my Secretary and a loo across the corridor. I remember them being a lovely pale apricot colour with nice chintz curtains. John Boland was Minister at the time and he wasn't a bit impressed with all the fuss being made for me. He had a wonderful political brain but a strange attitude about women's place in the scheme of things! I wouldn't brook any nonsense, so it was always fairly combative with him …

The Custom House was being renovated at the time with scaffolding and builders' rubble around the grounds. A few months into my junior ministry, John summoned me to a meeting on the lawn of the Custom House together with his private secretary and the Chairman of the Commissioners of the OPW. He pointed to a dead tree and litter everywhere and stated that he wanted it all removed by the following Monday. However, he'd forgotten that the Government had recently brought in a provision whereby each department could spend a limited amount on ongoing maintenance and repairs without going through the OPW. I immediately agreed with him that it was very unsightly and reminded him about the recent change and told him to clean it up himself from his own Department of Environment funds. I turned on my heels and left him seething beside two very embarrassed public officials. I had no more problems with him after that!

In making me a junior minister, the Taoiseach, Garret Fitzgerald had dropped my constituency colleague Michael D'Arcy, which really polarised the political situation within Fine Gael in Wexford. While I got re-elected at the next election, Michael lost his seat but at the subsequent election I lost my seat and Michael got his back, Fine Gael at all times retaining two seats out of five in the constituency. By then Brendan Howlin was on the pitch for Labour, and with three strong Fine Gael candidates with no real prospect of three seats again, the Fine Gael troops lined up on all sides. It was a very destructive sort of politics, going nowhere fast. I had always had a big interest in Europe and in the legislation coming from Brussels, so when the Party asked me to run in the European elections in 1999, I agreed and was successfully elected as an MEP.

Later on, and with my support, Eddie O'Reilly was selected as the third Fine Gael candidate at the selection convention ahead of the 2002 general election, but within weeks of that selection taking place, Fine Gael headquarters insisted that we drop him from the ticket, and that, much against my wishes, I stand again for the Dáil. It wasn't a clever move, and my opponents (inside and outside Fine Gael) went around saying, "She's a member of the European Parliament and the Senate and now she wants a third job!" I was hammered by my own and everyone else, but it didn't harm me in the long run. By the time the 2004 European elections came about, I got great support again in Wexford and was re-elected to Brussels. Mairead McGuinness was added late in the day, and again against all the odds, we got two out of the three seats in the constituency now called the East.

I found the European Parliament to be very refreshing. You're debating policy in areas in which you have great interest and often experience, and you can agree or disagree across the different political groups, unlike in Leinster House where the Party Whip must rule the day on most policy decisions, whether you agree with them or not. I was a member of the Environment, Public Health and Consumer Affairs Committee from day one, and also at different times on the Agricultural Committee and on the Industry, Research and Energy Committee. I was the European Parliament's Rapporteur on the Emissions Trading Directive, which is the basis of Europe's climate change policy. Several national delegations in my own EPP group seriously opposed it and after many months of tough and often acrimonious debate, I finally got it through the plenary session with overwhelming cross-party support. While it's far from perfect and still needs tightening, it is the largest Emissions Trading Scheme in the world today, and a prototype for what they're doing in North America, China and elsewhere.

I did a lot of other work in various areas, including a Report on the Veterinary Medicines Directive and battled for certain essential drugs on welfare grounds for horses. I was also on the Temporary Committee dealing with Foot and Mouth Disease and was the Rapporteur for the European Parliament on the Directive on Maximum Residue Levels – the residue level of drugs allowed in meat products in the food chain. I felt I was productive. I could grasp a brief well and do what had to be done. Every MEP has their own niche area, but the story often doesn't make the press at home.

> "I felt I was productive. I could grasp a brief well and do what had to be done."

I do however remember one incident that was widely reported. During the debate on the Lisbon Treaty, I was on my feet and about to speak on the outcome of the second referendum in Ireland when a racket started at the back of the chamber in Strasbourg. I turned around to see Nigel Farage of UKIP entering, followed by a group of people including one Irish independent MEP from Munster. They were all wearing green sweaters and pixie hats, dressed as leprechauns and jeering at the outcome of the Irish vote. I got quite exercised with them and they retreated rapidly!

For years I resisted the idea of quotas for women candidates as I worried that it would de-value the currency of any woman elected through such a system. Now I've come to the conclusion that the present legislation which has a sunset clause is probably the best balance and is needed. When I was elected to Wexford Corporation in 1974, I was the only woman on it, there had never been a woman Mayor before me and then within a couple of elections, two or three other women were elected and became Mayor of Wexford. I do believe that role models are important, and I hope that in a few short years, there won't be a need for quotas, as we will have reached a critical mass of female TDs and councillors coming organically through the selection and election systems in each constituency.

Irish Independent, 1988
Courtesy of Irish Newspaper Archive

When applying for a job you must first present your CV...

Mary Banotti's CV

- A nurse in Britain, the USA and Canada
- An aid worker in Africa.
- A welfare officer and community activist in Ireland.
- A mother raising a daughter alone.
- A legislator in the European parliament on environment, disability and the developing world.
- Co-founder of Women's Aid.
- Co-founder of the Rutland Centre for the treatment of alcoholism.

MARY Banotti

Banotti Campaign Headquarters 46 Dawson Street, Dublin 2. telephone 01 671 7244 fax 01 671 7490
email campaign@banotti.ie web site www.banotti.ie
If you would like to support or make a donation to the Mary Banotti campaign call 1850 346 342.

Westmeath Examiner, 1997
Courtesy of Irish Newspaper Archive

1981–1992 Pushing Politics to Deliver Rights For Women

> "At the time it was quite sexy to be a nuisance."

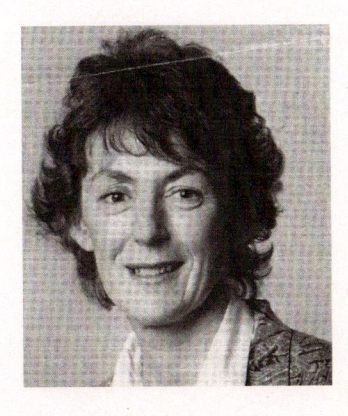

1984 MEP
Mary Banotti

Member of the European Parliament for Dublin 1984–2004

United Nations Population Fund (UNFPA) Goodwill Ambassador for Ireland 1999

Co-founder of Women's Aid

Chairwoman of The Rutland Centre

First female presidential candidate for Fine Gael

Intensely involved in politics all her life, Mary Banotti travelled widely throughout the 1950s and '60s, taking an avid interest in the social movements and events of the day. Having trained as a nurse in London, she worked her way around cities as diverse as Vancouver, New York, Nairobi and Rome, returning to Ireland in 1970 just as the Irish Women's Liberation Movement was beginning to make its mark. With daughter Tania in tow, Mary quickly immersed herself in the work of the movement, helping to establish both Women's Aid and the Rutland Centre.

Initial campaigns for a seat in the 1983 Senate and in the Dublin Central by-elections were not successful, but undaunted, the following year Mary secured a nomination to run in the elections for the European Parliament. She was elected to represent the constituency of Dublin in the European Parliament in 1984, a position she held until her retirement in 2004. She was the Fine Gael candidate in the presidential election of 1997, finishing second to Mary McAleese. Mary Banotti is the eldest sister of the former Fine Gael Deputy Leader and Minister for Justice, Nora Owen, and the grandniece of Michael Collins and Margaret Collins-O'Driscoll.

I come from a family with a strong political history, so wherever I went in the world I was always involved in the politics of the place in which I was living. I started looking out into a wider world in the 1950s. I rebelled and left home in 1958/59, went to London and trained as a nurse, while also running a stall in the Portobello Market. In 1961 I took myself off to Canada, and from there to America.

The world I found myself in was intensely political. I was there at the height of the civil rights movement and I was on my way home from work when I heard that John F. Kennedy had been shot. It was a seminal moment and I'll never forget it. I subsequently spent some time in Kenya as part of a medical team giving anti-measles vaccines and I met my husband who was a doctor there. We got married in Italy and my daughter Tania was born there.

After my marriage broke down I came back to Ireland in October 1970. I always say, somewhat dramatically, that it was as if my whole life up to then was a preparation for coming back to this newly emerging country. I remember watching the Late Late Show the night the women involved in the Women's Movement were being interviewed by Gay Byrne and I thought, "Wow! This is going to be really interesting". There were so many pressing needs and at the time it was quite sexy to be a nuisance. I very quickly joined the Women's Lib movement and got involved in all of that. At every demonstration we attended there was Tania tagging along with me in her little buggy. We set up Women's Aid and when we got a house from a developer in Harcourt Street we announced that there would be a refuge there. Within two days it was practically full.

My friendship with my sister Nora has been very important to me and the day she was elected was the happiest day of my life. We were out at the count and Nora was your classic middle-class housewife with three small children. She came up to me and said, "I think I'm going to be elected and I think I'm going to cry" and I said "Wow! We'll go outside, and we'll walk up and down." We came back in and then five minutes later she came over and said; "I think I'm going to be defeated" and we had to go outside again. Then she was elected, and I remember afterwards Tania and I driving home and singing the Dory Previn song "Twenty Mile Zone". It was amazing and wonderful.

Nora's husband Brian was terrific. He was really supportive of her, but not every one's husband was as helpful. I remember a number of women telling me that their own husbands deeply resented their involvement in politics because they felt it interfered with their own lives. In many ways it was almost easier for me because, even though I was caring for Tania, I didn't have to deal with that.

At the time of the Eighth Amendment in 1983 our brother was a solicitor working with Peter Sutherland. I remember him explaining to our mother the reasons why it was such a dangerous amendment. The day of the vote I was tired and upset. I went out to visit her and I asked her a question I'd never asked her in my entire life, "Mum, how did you vote?" She said, "I wrote undecided across my ballot paper." I burst into tears because this was a hugely radical gesture from somebody like her, a very devout Catholic who went to mass every day and spent her life trying to persuade all of us to go too.

In 1984 I was elected to the European Parliament. Right from the start I loved every minute. I didn't get too bogged down in worrying about it being really hard, partially because up to then I had led a fairly full life, so even if it sometimes was difficult, I just got on with it. In those days the Parliament was a really exciting place to be. I remember meeting some legendary older women there and it was great to hear their stories. The writer Alberto Moravio was

> "We set up Women's Aid and when we got a house from a developer in Harcourt Street we announced that there would be a refuge there. Within two days it was practically full."

part of our group and there was also a member of the von Stauffenberg family whose father was part of the plot to kill Hitler. Ian Paisley was there at that time too, jumping up and down and having a great time doing it.

I was lucky enough that on my first day in the European Parliament, of all the newcomers, my name was picked out of a hat to speak. Because the Parliament was multilingual I thought I'd deliver some of my speech in Irish, a little bit in English and end up in Italian. When I started to speak in Irish, the Chair practically started levitating. "Stop! Stop! I don't understand what you're saying. Kindly address the Parliament in one of the seven or eight official languages." I said, "I'm speaking my own language", then continued in Italian. The other people in the chamber burst out laughing because that particular Chair was very tough, and they were enjoying the sight of this new member sassing her. I ended up on every newspaper the next day, and from then on, I kind of had an instinct for it.

Throughout my time in Europe the issue of child abduction was a huge problem. People were approaching the Parliament for help and I was a member of the committee these requests were coming to. I decided to take the issue on board and make it my own. I worked very hard on it and in some ways, I think the fact that I was so publicly associated with it kept a focus on it and people took care that it didn't continue to happen. I also made it a big issue in America where I was appointed to the board of the American Centre for Missing and Abducted Children. I made good friends there and I did my best to make sure that our efforts in combatting child abduction were a success.

The presidential campaign in 1997 was a pretty nasty affair, particularly for some of the other candidates, and it seems to be only getting worse. I came a good second with almost 40% of the vote. After all that excitement I took a simple short break in Connemara and was then back to the Parliament after three days. I busied myself with my work there and keeping my constituents informed on the issues that were prevalent at the time.

I spent twenty years in the European Parliament and looking back on my time in politics, the things I'm most proud of are my involvement in setting up the Rutland Centre and the Women's Refuge in Dublin, the work I've done on abducted children in both Europe and America and trying to make an impact on behalf of my country in Europe. It was my life and perhaps it was our good fortune that at the time there were so many pressing issues to deal with.

PROUD TO SERVE: The Voices of the Women of Cumann na nGaedheal and Fine Gael 1922-1992

COUNCILLOR Therese Ahearn, Breda Allen, chairperson, Fine Gael National Women's Committee and Ann O'Connell at the strategy meeting.

Evening Herald, 1985
Courtesy of Irish Newspaper Archive

"Under the watchful eye of the European Court Irish Governments have been embarrassed and coerced into putting women on a par with men before the law."

1989 TD
Theresa Ahearn

Teachta Dála for Tipperary 1989-2000

Chair of the Oireachtas Joint Committee on Women's Affairs 1993-1995

Fine Gael Director of Elections in South Tipperary 1981-1982

Fine Gael Spokeswoman on Labour 1992, Energy 1992-1993, Equality and Disabilities 1997-2000

Committed equality advocate Theresa Ahearn grew up in a traditional rural household in Golden, Co Tipperary. She was first elected as a TD for Fine Gael in 1989 and throughout her time in the Dáil was Party Spokesperson on areas including energy, labour and women's affairs.

Similar to many of her peers, Theresa was inspired to join Fine Gael by Garret Fitzgerald. She attended her first party meeting in 1979, and for the first two years she was the only woman in the local organisation. Her tremendous organisational skills resulted in her quickly becoming Secretary of the District Council, and then Constituency Secretary. Later she became Fine Gael's first woman organiser, and she was the Party's Director of Elections in South Tipperary for each of the three elections that took place between 1981 and 1982. When Theresa expressed a desire to move out of backroom politics in 1983 and go into public life herself, her initiative was met with a distinct lack of enthusiasm. Her suggestion that she be co-opted to take the place of a local councillor who had died, was met with suggestions that her children were too young. Undeterred, she persevered and subsequently served as a public representative on South Tipperary County Council for six years.

Between 1993 and 1995 Theresa was Chair of the Oireachtas Joint Committee on Women's Affairs and her interests also included areas such as foreign affairs, enterprise and economic strategy. An energetic advocate for the promotion of rural development, Theresa was particularly pleased to see the establishment of the Tipperary Rural Business Development Institute.

The youngest of six children, Theresa's parents John and Catherine Scott were ardently committed to Fine Gael. In an interview with Úna Claffey in 1992, Theresa recalled that as a student living in Dublin, she was always guaranteed that a train ticket would arrive at election time to ensure she could travel home to Tipperary to cast that all-important vote for the Party.

Irish Farmers Journal, 1999
Courtesy of Irish Newspaper Archive

In that same interview Theresa observed that the dominant spirit growing up in the Scott household was one of egalitarianism, and her mother Catherine was determined that all three of her daughters would have an independent career. Theresa studied history, economics and maths at UCD, where one of her tutors was Garret Fitzgerald. After college she worked as a school teacher in Navan, before returning to her native county to teach maths at the Central Technical Institute in Tipperary. Theresa then got involved in the local branch of Macra na Feirme where she met her husband Liam. The couple settled in Clonmel and became parents to four children.

Theresa's commitment to equality resulted in her appointment as Fine Gael Spokeswoman on Equality and Disabilities, a position she held from 1997 until her death from cancer in 2000, at the age of forty-nine.

Theresa Ahearn was a strong advocate for women's rights and equality, as evidenced in the following speech, delivered two years after being first elected to the Dáil.

> "It has taken the tenacity, valour and obstinate determination of many women over the years to reverse the blatant discrimination against them in the laws."

1 May 1991

Private Members' Business - An Bille um an Aonú Leasú Déag ar an mBunreacht (Uimh. 3), 1991: An Dara Céim (atógáil)
Eleventh Amendment of the Constitution (No. 3) Bill, 1991: Second Stage (Resumed)

I warmly welcome and support this amendment to our Constitution proposed by my colleague, Deputy Gay Mitchell. As far as the women of Ireland are concerned, this amendment is long overdue. It is appropriate, and indeed important that we have a clear, unequivocal, unambiguous clause inserted into the Constitution underpinning the fact that women are indeed equal to men and must be so deemed under the laws of the State.

For far too long women have laboured, and sadly continue to labour, under an abundance of discriminatory attitudes, practices and even laws. It has taken the tenacity, valour and obstinate determination of many women over the years to reverse the blatant discrimination against them in the laws.

Joining the European Community gave a tremendous boost to the pursuit of equality for women under law. Fortunately the women's movement seized the opportunity presented by European Community membership to push Ireland into the 20th century as far as the issue of women's rights was concerned. Under the watchful eye of the European Court Irish Governments have been embarrassed and coerced into putting women on a par with men before the law. Now we urgently need to move forward, to put Ireland into the 21st century and take the all-important steps of publicly demonstrating through our Constitution that we as a Nation unreservedly acknowledge the inherent right to equality in the economic, political and social spheres.

The Constitution is the guiding light for all our laws. It is the soil in which the plant of our law is rooted. Yet, viewed from a woman's point of view, it is an unbalanced document. Women, wherever they get a mention, are by and large relegated exclusively to domestic spheres. No other role is readily seen for women. The language and thinking of the Constitution are male dominated. Yet is it not an ironic twist that remedies for some of the injustices against women have been arrived at by recourse to the Constitution? I share Deputy Mitchell's view that this is not good enough. There are ambiguities in the Constitution. The interpretation of certain Articles depends on the courts which may or may not choose to see inequality. Clearly Article 40.1 and 40.3 are most certainly not on every occasion seen by the courts to, without hesitation, support the notion of equality. As matters stand, the recognition of equality of women can be won or lost by the attitude to the Constitution by the courts.

I am not at all impressed by the Government's recital of all they are supposed to have done to improve the lot of women. Is it not scarcely a matter for self-congratulation that they have set about righting injustices against half the population? The fact that we still need an Oireachtas Joint Committee on Women's Rights serves to show that women do not yet enjoy full equality in all spheres. The very existence of this committee, and indeed the lack of a men's rights committee, speaks volumes of the position of women in Irish society in 1991.

If one takes a glance around this House or the Seanad or looks at the composition of the Cabinet one must ask, why are there so few women? The fact that there are thirteen women in the Dáil out of a total of 166 Members; six out of 60 in the Seanad and one out of 15 in the Cabinet is stark evidence that all is not well for women today.

PROUD TO SERVE: The Voices of the Women of Cumann na nGaedheal and Fine Gael 1922-1992

Our Target

A Minimum of 40% representation at all levels of Policy Making.

Between us we can make it happen!

JOIN WPA NOW!

Women's Political Association
Courtesy of Alan Kinsella, Irish Election Literature

1981-1992 Pushing Politics to Deliver Rights For Women

"Undoubtedly, having women representatives changes the agenda – for the better."

1989 SENATOR and TD
Helen Keogh

Senator 1989-1992; 1997-2002

Teachta Dála for Dun Laoghaire Rathdown 1992-1997

Spokeswoman on Equality, opportunity and The Family 2001-2002

President of the Women's Political Association

Helen Keogh joined the Women's Political Association in the early 1980s and quickly immersed herself in the campaigning work of the organisation. She got to know a number of women in politics, and in 1985 Mary Harney invited her to get involved with the nascent Progressive Democrats. Helen was an unsuccessful PD candidate at the 1987 general election, but was appointed to the Seanad two years later under the terms of the post 1989 election deal with Fianna Fáil. In 1992 she was elected TD for Dun Laoghaire-Rathdown, and after the loss of that seat in 1997, was again nominated to the Seanad as part of the PD deal with Fianna Fáil that year.

Helen left the PDs in 2000 and joined Fine Gael, where having unsuccessfully contested the 2002 Dáil and Seanad elections, she continued to hold the council seat she first won in 1991. Throughout her time in politics Helen worked hard to progress policy and shape developments on areas including women's rights, equality and justice. Her commitment to those issues continued to inform her subsequent work as CEO of the overseas aid agency World Vision.

The inspiration to get involved in politics came from my belief that women should be empowered and should be a vital part of society. My views were hugely influenced by both my parents. My mother was a nurse who worked at a time it seemed nobody else's mother worked. She was a very devout Catholic, who absolutely believed in women's rights, and my dad was always very supportive. The objective of the Women's Political Association was to encourage women to become active in public and political life, so I joined in the early 1980s, along with people like my good friend Frances Fitzgerald. Later I became President of the WPA and when I look back on it now, and all the fantastic women that I met, it's been a huge part of my life and who I am.

I canvassed for Monica Barnes in the 1982 election. The natural progression for me, had I thought of joining a political party, would have been to join Fine Gael, but at that time I was so taken up with work and family that that was something for the future. I knew quite a number of politicians through the WPA, one of whom was Mary Harney. In the summer of 1985 she told me they were thinking of setting up a new political party, and then that December she rang me and said, "We're launching this party tomorrow, will you come?" There was incredible enthusiasm that politics was going to be different and I wanted to help influence policy, particularly from a feminist perspective, so I became Chair of the Dun Laoghaire Constituency. The PDs ran three candidates there in 1987, Geraldine Kennedy got the seat and I was upset not to be one of the fourteen TDs that were elected that time. However, I learned a lot and got very involved in a backroom capacity. After the 1989 election, a deal was done to go into government with Fianna Fáil. It included three Senate seats and I couldn't believe it when I was appointed to one of them. It was a wonderful experience.

It's a great honour to represent people at both local and national level. I started on Dublin County Council and Dun Laoghaire Borough Council in the early 1990s, right in the middle of the development plan, and it was amazing to me that there wasn't more joined up thinking, there were many vested interests at play. With much talk of corruption, people asked, "Did you see brown paper envelopes being passed?" I didn't and my naïve assumption was that people wouldn't do that. By the next development plan, thanks to the PDs, there was legislation passed that made the more corrupt practices less possible. Dun Laoghaire is the most liberal constituency in the country and so when plans were drawn up to settle or provide halting sites for Travellers I naïvely assumed that most people would support them. It was disappointing to come across so much of the NIMBY attitude. I'm proud that I voted for the plan for Travellers, however, it was not implemented in full due to objections – a very short term view.

Amongst the most important legislation I was engaged with while in the PDs was the equality legislation then Minister Mervyn Taylor was working on, which was eventually overturned by the President on advice. That was when the committee system was really coming into its own and it was the kind of consensus politics that I believe in. There was a lot of hard work behind the scenes trying to get it to be the best it could possibly be. At that time also we became aware of the awful sexual abuse cases which were coming to light. We didn't realise the extent or how pervasive it was but I am glad that I played some part in focussing attention on cases, bringing questions to the floor and seeking justice. The injustice also of the X case was very important to me and was something I was particularly vociferous about. I also campaigned vigorously on the divorce referendum. It is very satisfying to see the important advances that have been made over the years, built on decades of effort.

I was appointed to the Seanad again in 1997 and that was an unhappy time in politics for me. By that stage the PDs were very chastened, but still doing deals. I remember we were told at a parliamentary party meeting that Ray Burke was

> "If you're going to be successful in politics you have to be really focused."

going to be appointed a minister, and I said it was like death by a thousand cuts. Despite working very hard as spokesperson on a number of briefs, I felt bogged down and disillusioned and didn't feel that I could bring as much in relation to policy as I might have wished. Monica was one of the people I confided in at that time and she inspired me to join Fine Gael.

If you're going to be successful in politics you have to be really focused and that can exclude everything else. Around that time of upheaval my invalid parents were living with us and then passed away within nine months of each other which I found difficult to deal with especially when politics is so all-encompassing. If you're a young woman with a family it's as demanding as any career but even less family friendly. During my time in the Oireachtas, the majority of women either did not have children or had older children. As with a very few others, when I first ran our children were very young, my parents were still in the whole of their health and supportive, I had the most incredible husband in Paddy, and a very good childminder. Like so much in life, it's all brilliant until it doesn't work and then it's catastrophic, or so you feel.

I think for all of us getting elected was a great accomplishment. I have a copy of the photograph commemorating the Oireachtas Women 1918 - 2008 taken in the Dáil chamber. Just look at the number of (living) women involved over those ninety years and what proportion of the Dáil chamber it takes up. It's just over one a year. You have to find a way to re-dress the balance and that's why I really believe in quotas. Look at all the fantastic women who are there now, but we need more. I remember in 2002 it seemed that there was a breakthrough with more women than ever before elected. Gay Byrne had us all on the Late Late Show. He asked us *"who minds your children?"* I was a bit taken aback. Part of me wanted to say, *"That's none of your business"*, but I didn't, I really regret that! The only one who did challenge him was Liz McManus from Labour who said, *"I don't know why you're asking us this. If it was men here, you wouldn't be asking this question."*

I am very proud of my work in the Women's Political Association, inspiring a number of women to get involved, ensuring that women's voices are heard and that it's an equal voice, not just from the side-lines. It shows that without any kind of a political background you can make the transition from being an activist to being somebody who is part and parcel of the political establishment, in the sense of driving the agenda politically, contributing to society and showing the way for women. I see myself very much as a facilitator and within the Fine Gael Party I worked hard to help shape attitudes, particularly on the abortion issue. Women in the Party continue to do that and it's very important in shaping policy now and for the future. Undoubtedly, having women representatives changes the agenda – for the better.

PROUD TO SERVE: The Voices of the Women of Cumann na nGaedheal and Fine Gael 1922-1992

Image courtesy of Mary Jackman

"I felt privileged to be part of that force of women. Even then I would have been aware that we were all very different, but it's good to have a mix."

1989 SENATOR
Mary Jackman

Senator 1989–1993, 1997–2002

First female Cathaoirleach Limerick County Council

First female public representative from Limerick elected to the Seanad

Member of the Joint Committee on Women's Rights 1989–1992

Member of the Joint Committee on Health and Children 1997

Mary Jackman was first elected to Limerick County Council in 1985, going on to become its first female Cathaoirleach in 1998. When she secured a seat on the Labour panel in 1989 she became the first female public representative from Limerick to be elected to Seanad Éireann. She lost that seat in 1993, but subsequently returned to the Seanad from 1997 to 2002.

Throughout her political career, Mary was unsuccessful in a number of attempts to enter Dáil Éireann, narrowly missing the mark in 1997 when she lost out by just over three hundred votes. A secondary school teacher, she was a member of the Joint Committee on Women's Rights from 1989 to 1992 and the Joint Committee on Health and Children in 1997.

I always felt that Fine Gael were very pro-women, but when I was first elected to Limerick County Council there were very few women there. I'd say there were only two or three women out of the whole thirty and for a good while I was the only Fine Gael woman in the Council. We were very much country people and the interesting thing about my background is that my father's side were very strong Fine Gael supporters and my mother's side were roaring Fianna Fáil. I always say "roaring Fianna Fáil" because they were the real roaring ones and it didn't always make for the best recipe. My father was a farmer and he was mad on politics and very involved in the Irish Creamery Milk Supplier Association (ICMSA). My grandfather on my mother's side was Chairperson of Limerick County Council, but even so, all my mother's family voted for me when I ran for the Dáil.

I remember when I was in the Council one guy used to give me a hard time about that. *"I don't know what you're doing here, sure all belonging to you are Fianna Fáil."* I'd get that at every meeting, it was like the last mystery of the

Rosary. Thinking about it now I was worse to take heed of him, but I couldn't stick this carry on. I'd give as good as I'd get and throw the odd scud missile at him. You would have to because they didn't know how to deal with women, even the council officials, because they were so used to men until we appeared.

I got great encouragement from people like Ted Russell in Fine Gael when I first started out on the Senate trail. He was a former Mayor of Limerick, a TD and a Senator and he sat me down and said, *"This is what you do now."* He had this little notebook of contacts going back years and he told me that instead of going in asking people to give you their vote it was more important to interact with them and see how they were doing. That's what it's all about really.

People around here would have known me because I was a secondary school teacher in Presentation, Sexton Street in Limerick. When you get into this political business, your supporters get very involved in the person. I was never questioned about being a woman. As far as they were concerned I was going to do the job and that was the end of it. I didn't think in terms of male and female and I wouldn't call myself a feminist but I really felt, why couldn't I do it? I was off on a trot and the same with the other women at that time. We just took off and the men who came and canvassed with me were just fabulous.

I kind of consider that an idyllic period in my life. I did every single county and I was gone for six weeks. I got the greatest chances to see the country and to meet lots of great people and I didn't think in terms of a woman going off driving on her own. They loved to see a woman coming, maybe because women were rare at that time. They were so welcoming and sometimes a person would meet you and introduce you to the various different people. I remember visiting one guy, who said *"Speak to me!"* so I stood up and after a whole big spiel, all he said was *"I like you Mary"* and out the door I was sent. When I was elected they were all delighted because there were so few women. Afterwards I went around and thanked them for their support.

Irish people are extremely political so for anyone coming into politics now, the first thing I'd say is that it's important that they have an understanding of what it entails. People are nice and genuine but the Irish psyche tends to give *"Harvey Smiths"* to politicians. That's a crude way of putting it but they do, so you either do it well or you don't. I was very disappointed not to get elected to the Dáil. I think I was only beaten by a handful of votes one time, but you get over that. It was a period where women were not looked up to really and when you'd knock on the doors you'd get an awful lot of slagging and "What is she doing coming in here now?" It was a kind of transition period but I always found great interaction once you would sit and chat and ask how they were doing. I was enjoying it, I wasn't even thinking of the politics.

The Seanad was quite civilised, there was some very intelligent discussion and I loved that it wasn't all about your man down the road and getting him this and that. There were Seanadóirí that would have come from all walks of life who knew what they were at, and being a teacher, I was very interested in

> *"We were in the feministic ring without realising that we were feminists and I mean why shouldn't we go and do what we had to do? Nobody ever said, 'I won't vote for you because you are a woman'."*

educational matters. There was great camaraderie, we learned from each other and I found it very exciting.

We had a lot of good women, but there were so few, I'd say only about 12 or 13% then. To me, Nuala Fennell and Monica Barnes were the feminists of Fine Gael and Ireland. They were bright, they had everything prepared and they knew what they were talking about. They were outspoken and serious about what they were doing; they'd say what they had to say, and nothing fazed them. I thought that Madeleine Taylor-Quinn was brilliant, she would give as good as she got, Gemma Hussey did an awful lot for education and I adored Monica Barnes. She was so solid. I felt privileged to be part of that force of women. Even then I would have been aware that we were all very different, but it's good to have a mix. As far as I'm concerned, they were really bright sparks. They were fine women, we had great craic and I learned a lot from them.

I think that group of us was the start of a turnabout in the political scene. It was the first time you had that level of women involved. We were in the feministic ring without realising that we were feminists and I mean why shouldn't we go and do what we had to do? Nobody ever said, "*I won't vote for you because you are a woman*". For me it was a journey and I just kind of felt that this is what we all should be doing. You might say that it was the cusp of things beginning to change, and from there I think women blossomed.

Women who dare to band together

Frances Fitzgerald TD defends the right of women to form their own group in the Dail, up to recently a men's club

THE CHEEK of us Women TDs - daring to form a group in Dail Eireann. Daring to think we had something in common which could usefully be shared and pooled. Being daft enough to think that our experience might collectively accelerate the breakdown of some of the barriers to women's participation in politics.

Over the past week or so, I've read with amusement and a little disappointment the almost hysterical reaction from some quarters to this small initiative by women members of Dail Eireann, the formation of the 84 Group.

Let me spell out the concept. It falls within the ambit of "positive action" which assuredly will underpin many of the recommendations of the forthcoming Second Report of the Commission on the Status of Women to be published on Thursday. The 84 Group is positive action, a measure of the commitment of those of us who have achieved election to ensure that in future the particular experience of women can be brought to bear on an institution which has, since its inception been almost entirely male.

Having thought about some of the criticisms, I realise that they can be summarised as the "why don't you just roll up your sleeves and get stuck in there and be one of the boys" school of thought on "Women in Politics". The idea requires that you believe that there is nothing wrong with the way the system is organised or how the process of government works — just that we women have to learn it. The "male as norm" approach.

One commentator in recent days referred dismissively to the group of women TDs sitting round discussing the appalling situation faced by women in the former Yugoslavia and, in an attempt to prove the error of our judgment that women had a special concern, pointed to the work of Ministers Andrews and Spring raising the issue at an international level. Ah yes, one swallow.

□ The 84 Group

Certainly, as one would expect from two thoughtful politicians, they have represented Ireland well on the issue — but that this disproves the need for positive action by women TDs on issues such as rape must have come as quite a surprise to women right around the country.

It ignores the fact that it has been a long struggle by rape crisis centres and women's refuges in this country to achieve even basic recognition, let alone funding, for their essential services, and to begin to force into public consciousness the fact that violence against women is criminal. That struggle is far from over.

Women in Dail Eireann constitute just 12pc of the total membership. Research shows that in such imbalanced situations (and the same would apply if the male-female balance were reversed) there is a need for a critical mass of around one-third if the perspectives of both groups are to be included and respected fully.

SO WE have a long way to go and, as those who have been elected, we owe it to other women to work to make the structures more workable for women. We also owe it to women and to men to ensure that on many issues where women's experience is different from and complementary to men's, that we contribute to that experience.

Sometimes the most effective way of doing that will be as a collective voice.

We've met for about one-and-a-half hours at this stage and a leading academic is talking about "big sister." Meanwhile, we see Fitzwilliam Lawn Tennis Club, a sports club, supporting rather than redressing the misogyny in our society. There is no comparison.

I am also amused by the notion that we would have reacted strongly against the men in Dail Eireann setting up a club — amused because the commentators do not see the irony of their remarks. Dail Eireann has been a men's club until recently.

I am, perhaps, most amused by the suggestion that as a group we had set ourselves up as some sort of marginal or parallel body to the exclusion of our responsibilities within the Dail. Can I remind those with such concerns that we number among us five Ministers or Minister of State, members of local authorities, party executives and soon, I hope, we will be participating in the new Dail Committees. As well, we work in our constituencies and communities.

Be assured, our once-monthly meetings will not distract us — as women who have more than proved our capacity as competent organisers and representatives in so many different ways. The 84 Group exists because it is an important and necessary step in accelerating progress to real equality.

Irish Independent, 1993
Courtesy of Irish Newspaper Archive

1981–1992 Pushing Politics to Deliver Rights For Women

"Ireland is an unfinished democracy."

1992 TD, SENATOR and MEP
Frances Fitzgerald

Teachta Dála for Dublin South-East 1992–1997, 1997–2002

Senator 2007–2011

Teachta Dála for Dublin Mid-West 2011–2016, 2016–2019

Member of the European Parliament for Dublin 2019–

Minister for Children and Youth Affairs 2011–2014

Minister for Justice and Equality 2014–2016; 2016–2017

Tánaiste 2016–2017

Tánaiste and Minister for Business, Enterprise and Innovation 2017

The longest serving female Fine Gael Minister

The only female Fine Gael Tánaiste to date

Frances Fitzgerald MEP first came to national prominence through her work as Chair of the National Women's Council in the late 1980s. She was elected to the Dáil in the general elections of 1992 and 1997, later winning a seat in the Seanad in 2007, where she became Leader of the Fine Gael group.

Returning to the Dáil at the 2011 general election, Frances served as Minister for Children and Youth Affairs until 2014, when she was appointed Minister for Justice and Equality. Following the general election of 2016, she was re-appointed to that position and simultaneously served as Tánaiste. In her seven years as a minister she introduced twenty-seven pieces of legislation, as well as facilitating the Marriage Equality and Children's referendums.

In June 2017 she was appointed Tánaiste and Minister for Business, Enterprise and Innovation. In November 2017 she resigned these posts in the face of opposition threats to bring down the Government based on accusations related to controversies emerging from An Garda Síochána. These accusations were subsequently dismissed by the Disclosures Tribunal report in October 2018. The Tribunal vindicated Frances, Judge Charleton describing her actions as "selfless".

Frances represented the constituency of Dublin Mid-West, is the longest serving female Fine Gael Minister and the only female Fine Gael Tánaiste to date. Frances was elected as a member of the European Parliament in 2019, and has been elected as EPP Co-ordinator for the European Parliament's Women's Rights Committee.

I've spent my life, inside and outside politics, working for equality, women's health and children's rights.

When I was in the Women's Council I initiated the Second Commission on the Status of Women. Under its Chair, Judge Mella Carroll an inspiring figure, we published a report which laid down key changes required by our changing society. Ireland, in three decades, has, as a result of her work and of the work of many members of women's organisations, changed from an inward-looking, rigid and controlling society riven by contempt for women and restriction of their rights. It has been fascinating to see issues I fought for from the outside becoming mainstream. Aspirations have become rights and Ireland has become one of the most open and accepting societies in the world.

That's a stunning transformation from the Ireland I experienced as a student of social science in UCD. To continue those studies at the LSE I went to live in London where I had my first child and served as a social worker. In London I didn't know many young mums in my area and I connected with the local branch of the National Childbirth Trust and met other new mothers through a local women's group in my area.

When I returned to Dublin with a new baby, I set up a similar group here. My other two sons were born in Dublin. It was my first experience of the strength women can represent once they decide on collective action. I worked as a social worker in Ballymun for ten years and joined the Women's Political Association out of my interest in equality issues.

But collective action in a suburban area can go only so far, and as my feminism strengthened, I realised only political engagement could achieve the raft of reform needed for women and children. I found Garret Fitzgerald inspiring, so I wrote to him in 1985 and said I'd like to join Fine Gael. I developed a good profile through my work as Chair of the Women's Council and in 1992 Garret asked me to run for election.

I didn't come from a political family, so I had to learn the art and the trade on the job. Mark Fitzgerald and the late Jim Mitchell offered solid advice on how to run a campaign. I was elected – to one of the most sexist and misogynistic institutions of the time. Some of that sexism was generational, mainly from older men who had been brought up in a different era. The evidence was everywhere: I might say something at Cabinet, or at the Parliamentary party. Some man would say the same thing. The Chair or another man would then quote what the man said, never referencing what a woman said. I learned quickly not to take it personally, but never to let it go unchallenged, either. The fact that bias is unconscious doesn't make it acceptable. Whether it appears in politics, media, academia or sport, it must be fought.

Everybody going into politics with an equality mission assumes that when progress is made, it will be permanent. We must learn that this rarely happens. The march of equality tends to be two steps forward, one step back. For

"But, no matter what the challenges, no matter how often progress is uneventful and equality forced to take a backward step, the fact is that politics is where reality is crafted out of hopes and dreams."

example, at one stage when I was Minister for Justice, women were in the five top positions in law. While it's an important marker that there were women experienced enough to break through, it is striking that each of us was replaced by a man. There wasn't a pipeline of women there to replace us. We've had two female Presidents and four female Tánaistes but the current reality is that 78% of representatives in the Dáil are male. We must be wary of wild enthusiasm about the firsts or the breakthroughs and concentrate on the fragility of the representation.

Women in politics face barriers in relation to childcare, cash and political culture so you need to have a more supportive system to encourage women to get involved. Mentoring is important and it's helpful for women that there are stricter laws about spending now. When Phil Hogan initially introduced quotas, we were already almost at 20%. I pushed that figure from 20 to 30%. The Party went out and really worked to get the numbers, but there's still not a critical mass. Too many women have been in the Senate and in the Dáil for one term and then gone. It's a tough, challenging business.

I now believe that we need a 50% female Cabinet, and I don't think you have to wait until there are 50% women in the Dáil. That's a new position for me but I've got to the point where I'm sick of it automatically being men and I'm tired of seeing poorer quality men getting positions ahead of higher quality women. My experience is that women contribute in a slightly different way. They're more reflective, less hierarchical and they like to open things up. I've been in one Cabinet with two women and a female Attorney General and I've been in a Cabinet with five women, and it does make a difference. It's good to have the variety and you can no longer run a country with one gender.

Ever since my time as Chair of the Women's Council I wanted to change what was going on with young people in St Patrick's Institute for Young Offenders, so closing that institution was very satisfying. The legislation on the Sexual Offences Act was hard fought and it's going to take a while to really settle in and show its worth, but it was important to give the message to young men that they cannot buy sex. As the first Minister for Children, I had a unique opportunity to establish the Department of Children and Youth Affairs, bring forward the Children's Referendum and change the Constitution. As Minister for Justice I changed the law in many areas: I established the Charities Regulatory Authority, the Legal Services Regulatory Authority, wrote the legislation for marriage equality through the Dáil and Seanad and strengthened the law on sexual offences.

I think the worst thing in the world is to exclude people and so I was thrilled to see the result of the Marriage Referendum. The evening I completed the marriage equality legislation in the Seanad with a packed gallery was a very emotional moment. That's a moment I will cherish forever.

Combining the highest level of political office with family life is extraordinarily challenging. I am very glad that when I got the opportunity to be a minister my family was reared. I spent twelve years in front bench opposition politics in six different portfolios, so I haven't much time for the highly adversarial nature of the Dáil. At times, opposition can be about headline-generation and while a "head on a plate" demand will always deliver headlines it doesn't – as the Charleton Tribunal proved – always deliver justice or fairness. I've paid a high political price for the exaggeration and inaccuracies of that approach.

That's life and it shows you how challenging politics is.

But, no matter what the challenges, no matter how often progress is uneventful and equality forced to take a backward step, the fact is that politics is where reality is crafted out of hopes and dreams.

BIBLIOGRAPHY
Primary and Secondary Sources

1. INTERVIEWS
Interview with Mary Banotti, July 2018
Interview with Myra Barry, August 2018
Interview with Deirdre Bolger, August 2018
Interview with Katharine Bulbulia, August 2018
Interview with Avril Doyle, August 2018
Interview with Frances Fitzgerald, July 2018 and November 2018
Interview with Mary Flaherty, August 2018
Interview with Mary Jackman, September 2018
Interview with Gemma Hussey, June 2018
Interview with Miriam Kearney, August 2018
Interview with Helen Keogh, August 2018
Interview with Nora Owen, June 2018
Interview with Madeleine Taylor-Quinn, June 2018
Interview with Noeleen Smith and Mary McKiernan, October 2018
Interview with Garret Ahearn, November 2018
Interview with Sarah Barnes, November 2018
Interview with Ann Marie Burke Browne, February 2019
Interview with Pól Ó Murchú, November 2018
Interview with Anthony Lawlor, November 2018
Interview with Garrett Fennell, December 2018
Interview with Vincent Blake, November 2018

2. SPEECHES*/FIRST HAND ACCOUNTS
Contributions to debates in the Dáil and the Seanad were accessed online via Oireachtas.ie

Theresa Ahearn
Oireachtas.ie. (2018). *Dáil Éireann debate - Wednesday, 1 May 1991*. [online] Available at: https://www.oireachtas.ie/en/debates/debate/dail/1991-05-01/24/#spk_638 [Accessed 6 Oct. 2018].

Monica Barnes
Barnes, Sarah and Hennessey Ailbhe, Notes from Recording with Monica Barnes April 2018 Unpublished, 2018.

Kathleen Browne
Oireachtas.ie. (2018). *Seanad Éireann debate - Wednesday, 19 Mar 1930*. [online] Available at: https://www.oireachtas.ie/en/debates/debate/seanad/1930-03-19/speech/26/ [Accessed 16 Sept. 2018]

Oireachtas.ie. (2018). *Seanad Éireann debate - Thursday, 12 Dec 1935*. [online] Available at: https://www.oireachtas.ie/en/debates/debate/seanad/1935-12-12/speech/9/ [Accessed 16 Sept. 2018]

Joan Burke
Oireachtas.ie. (2019). *Dáil Éireann debate - Thursday, 27 Mar 1980* [online] Available at: https://www.oireachtas.ie/en/debates/debate/dail/1980-03-27/speech/140/

Oireachtas.ie. (2019). *Dáil Éireann debate - Wednesday, 31 Mar 1971* [online] Available at: https://www.oireachtas.ie/en/debates/debate/dail/1971-03-31/speech/622/ [Accessed 4 Jan. 2019].

Margaret Collins-O'Driscoll
Oireachtas.ie. (2018). *Dáil Éireann debate - Friday, 20 Apr 1928* [online] Available at: https://www.oireachtas.ie/en/debates/debate/dail/1928-04-20/speech/158/ [Accessed 5 May 2018].

Eileen Costello
Witness Statement, The Bureau of Military History, M.A. W.S 1184 [online] Available at: http://www.bureauofmilitaryhistory.ie/reels/bmh/BMH.WS1184.pdf
[Accessed: 15 Oct. 2018]

Oireachtas.ie. (2019). *Seanad Éireann debate - Friday, 8 Apr 1927*. [online] https://www.oireachtas.ie/en/debates/debate/seanad/1927-04-08/speech/59/ [Accessed: 15 Oct. 2018]

Oireachtas.ie. (2018). *Seanad Éireann debate - Thursday, 17 Dec 1925*. [online] https://www.oireachtas.ie/en/debates/debate/seanad/1925-12-17/speech/14/ [Accessed: 16 Oct. 2018]

Nuala Fennell

Fennell, Nuala, *Political Woman, A Memoir*, Dublin, Currach Press, 2009.

Oireachtas.ie. (2018).

Dáil Éireann debate - Wednesday, 8 Jul 1992 [online] Available at: https://www.oireachtas.ie/en/debates/debate/dail/1992-07-08/speech/121/ [Accessed 25 Nov. 2018].

Alice Glenn

Oireachtas.ie. (2019). *Dáil Éireann debate - Friday, 29 Nov 1985*. [online] Available at: https://www.oireachtas.ie/en/debates/debate/dail/1985-11-29/3/#spk_33 [Accessed 19 Oct. 2018].

Oireachtas.ie. (2019). *Dáil Éireann debate - Tuesday, 25 Feb 1986*. [online] Available at: https://www.oireachtas.ie/en/debates/debate/dail/1986-02-25/21/#spk_159 [Accessed 19 Oct. 2018].

Irish Election Literature. (2019). *The Alice Glenn Report May 1986- 'A Woman voting for Divorce is like a Turkey voting for Christmas'*. [online] Available at: https://irishelectionliterature.com/2009/09/10/the-alice-glenn-report-may-1986/ [Accessed 19 Oct. 2018].

Glenn, A. (1986). *Why Fine Gael Divorced Alice Glenn*. [online] Irishelectionliterature.files.wordpress.com. Available at: https://irishelectionliterature.files.wordpress.com/2009/11/alice1a.jpg [Accessed 7 Feb. 2019]. [Accessed 19 Oct. 2018].

Brigid Hogan-O'Higgins

Oireachtas.ie. (2018). *Dáil Éireann debate – 1 Dec, 1976* [online] Available at: https://www.oireachtas.ie/en/debates/debate/dail/1976-12-01/speech/12/ [Accessed 5 Dec. 2018].

Patsy Lawlor

Lawlor, Patsy, (1976) "The Three Dimensional Role of Women", Address given at the ICA Summer Council Meeting, Killeshin House, Portlaoise Co. Laois, 14 July 1976. Records of the Irish Countrywomen's Association, NLI MS 39, 349.

Bridget Redmond

Oireachtas.ie. (2018). *Dáil Éireann debate - Tuesday, 20 May 1947*. [online] Available at: https://www.oireachtas.ie/en/debates/debate/dail/1947-05-20/speech/333/ [Accessed 25th Sept. 2018].

Mary Reynolds

Election address from Mrs. M Reynolds, *The Sligo Champion*, 8 May 1954.

Alice Stopford Green

Oireachtas.ie. (2019). *Seanad Éireann debate - Wednesday, 26 Nov 1924*. [online] https://www.oireachtas.ie/en/debates/debate/seanad/1924-11-26/speech/72/ [Accessed 22 Jan. 2019].

Mary Walsh

Oireachtas.ie. (2018). *Seanad Éireann debate – 4 Feb, 1976* [online] Available at: https://www.oireachtas.ie/en/debates/debate/seanad/1976-02-04/3/ [Accessed 7 Oct. 2018].

Jennie Wyse Power

Oireachtas.ie. (2018). *Seanad Éireann debate - Thursday, 17 Dec 1925*. [online] https://www.oireachtas.ie/en/debates/debate/seanad/1925-12-17/speech/38/ [Accessed 7 Sept. 2018].

Oireachtas.ie. (2018). *Seanad Éireann debate - Thursday, 17 Dec 1925*. [online] https://www.oireachtas.ie/en/debates/debate/seanad/1925-12-17/speech/46/ [Accessed 7 Sept. 2018].

Oireachtas.ie. (2018). *Seanad Éireann debate - Wednesday, 30 Mar 1927*. [online] https://www.oireachtas.ie/en/debates/debate/seanad/1927-03-30/speech/27/ [Accessed 7 Sept. 2018].

3. REFERENCES AND NOTES

Theresa Ahearn
1. Claffey, Úna, *The Women Who Won: Women of the 27th Dáil*, Dublin, Attic Press, 1993, p102.
2. ibid, p106.
3. Interview with Garret Ahearn, November 2018.
4. Oireachtas.ie. (2018). *Dáil Éireann debate - Wednesday, 1 May 1991*. [online] Available at: https://www.oireachtas.ie/en/debates/debate/dail/1991-05- 01/24/#spk_638 [Accessed 6 Oct. 2018].

Monica Barnes
1. Collins, Liam, Obituary - Monica Barnes, *Sunday Independent*, 6th May 2018, https://www.independent.ie/irish-news/obituary-monica-barnes-36878049 html) [Accessed 8 May 2018].
2. Interview with Sarah Barnes November 2018.
3. Barnes, Sarah and Hennessey Ailbhe, Notes from Recording with Monica Barnes, April 2018 Unpublished, 2018.

Kathleen Browne
1. Browne, Bernard. "*Kathleen A. Browne*." The Past: The Organ of the UÃ Cinsealaigh Historical Society, no. 32, 2016, pp. 108–115. www.jstor.org/stable/26202849. [Accessed 16 Sept. 2018].
2. McAuliffe, Mary, *Senator Kathleen A Browne, 1876 – 1943, Patriot, Politician and Practical Farmer*, Tipperary, Roscrea Publications, 2008.
3. Wright, Brendan, Biography, Kathleen Browne Festival, www.kathleenbrownefestival.net [online] Available at: https://kathleenbrownefestival.net/biography-2/ [Accessed 22 Oct. 2018].
4. Oireachtas.ie. (2018). *Seanad Éireann debate - Wednesday, 19 Mar 1930*. [online] Available at: https://www.oireachtas.ie/en/debates/debate/seanad/1930-03-19/speech/26/ [Accessed 16 Sept. 2018].
5. Oireachtas.ie. (2018). *Seanad Éireann debate - Thursday, 12 Dec 1935*. [online] Available at: https://www.oireachtas.ie/en/debates/debate/seanad/1935-12-12/speech/9/ [Accessed 16 Sept. 2018].

Joan Burke
1. Kelly, Darragh, An Appreciation: Joan Burke, *The Irish Times*, 5th Dec, 2016 [online] Available at: https://www.irishtimes.com/life-and-style/people/an-appreciation-joan-burke-1.2890885 [Accessed 6 May 2018].
2. Oireachtas.ie. (2019). *Dáil Éireann debate - Thursday, 27 Mar 1980* [online] Available at: https://www.oireachtas.ie/en/debates/debate/dail/1980-03-27/speech/140/ [Accessed 6 May 2018].
3. Interview with Ann Marie Burke Brown, February 2019.
4. Oireachtas.ie. (2019). *Dáil Éireann debate - Wednesday, 31 Mar 1971* [online] Available at: https://www.oireachtas.ie/en/debates/debate/dail/1971-03-31 speech/622/ [Accessed 4 Jan. 2019].

Margaret Collins-O'Driscoll
1. Election results Christopher Took and Sean Donnelly. Available at: https://electionsireland.org/candidate.cfm?ID=1252&sort=date&office=yes [Accessed 18 May 2018].
2. Information supplied by Pól Ó Murchú, grandson of Margaret Collins-O'Driscoll
3. Extract from the Dictionary of Irish Biography, cited on the Oireachtas website [online] Available at: https://beta.oireachtas.ie/en/visit-and-learn/votail-100-pioneers-in-parliamentary-politics/ [Accessed 5 May 2018].
4. Oireachtas.ie. (2018). *Dáil Éireann debate - Friday, 20 Apr 1928* [online] Available at: https://www.oireachtas.ie/en/debates/debate/dail/1928-04-20/speech/158/ [Accessed 5 May 2018].

Eileen Costello
1. Witness Statement, The Bureau of Military History, M.A. W.S 1184 [online] Available at: http://www.bureauofmilitaryhistory.ie/reels/bmh/BMH.WS1184.pdf [Accessed 15 Oct. 2018].
2. Tuam Town Commissioners Minutes, 1843 -1968 TTC/1/ A Descriptive List prepared by Galway County Council Archives (2014) p iv [online] Available at: http://gccapps.galwaycoco.ie/ArchivedDocuments/Tuam%20Town%20Commissioners%20&%20 Council%20-%20Minutes,%20TTC-1/TTC%2 Tuam%20Town%20Commissioners,%20Minutes,%20 Descriptive%20List TTC-1%20Tuam%20Town%20Commissioners,%20Minutes,%20Descriptive%2 List.pdf [Accessed 15 Oct. 2018].

3. Oireachtas.ie. (2018). *Seanad Éireann debate - Friday, 8 Apr 1927*. [online] https://www.oireachtas.ie/en/debates/debate/seanad/1927-04-08/speech/59/ [Accessed 15 Oct. 2018].

4. Oireachtas.ie. (2018). *Seanad Éireann debate - Thursday, 17 Dec 1925*. [online] https://www.oireachtas.ie/en/debates/debate/seanad/1925-12-17/speech/14/ [Accessed 16 Oct. 2018].

Nuala Fennell

1. Fennell, Nuala, *Political Woman, A Memoir*, Dublin, Currach Press, 2009 p.42

2. Ibid, pp 46-47

3. Ibid, p. 95

4. Interview with Garrett Fennell, December 2018.

5. Oireachtas.ie. (2018). *Dáil Éireann debate - Wednesday, 8 Jul 1992* [online] Available at: https://www.oireachtas.ie/en/debates/debate/dail/1992-07-08/speech/121/ [Accessed 25 Nov. 2018].

Alice Glenn

1. Lynch, M. (1984). Martin Lynch Interviews Alice Glenn. *Futureline*. [online] Available at: https://irishelectionliterature.com/tag/alice-glenn/ [Accessed 19 Oct. 2018].

2. Ibid

3. Irish Election Literature. (2018). *Leaflet from Alice Glenn, John Colgan, Michael Keating- Fine Gael- November 1982 Dublin Central*. [online] Available at: https://irishelectionliterature.com/2011/12/19/leaflet-from-alice-glenn-john-colgan-michael-keating-fine-gael-november-1982-dublin-central/ [Accessed 19 Oct.2018].

4. Ibid

5. Oireachtas.ie. (2018). *Dáil Éireann debate - Friday, 29 Nov 1985*. [online] Available at: https://www.oireachtas.ie/en/debates/debate/dail/1985-11-29/3/#spk_33 [Accessed 19 Oct. 2018].

6. Irish Election Literature. (2018). *The Alice Glenn Report May 1986- 'A Woman voting for Divorce is like a Turkey voting for Christmas'*. [online] Available at: https://irishelectionliterature.com/2009/09/10/the-alice-glenn-report-may-1986/ [Accessed 19 Oct. 2018].

7. Glenn, A. (1986). *Why Fine Gael Divorced Alice Glenn*. [online] Irishelectionliterature.files.wordpress.com. Available at: https:/irishelectionliterature.files.wordpress.com/2009/11/alice1a.jpg [Accessed 19 Oct. 2018].

8. *The Irish Times*. (2011). Conviction politician whose patriotism was defined by her faith. [online] Available at: https://www.irishtimes.com/life-and-style/peopleconviction-politician-whose-patriotism-was-defined-by-her-faith-1.15560 [Accessed 19th Oct. 2018].

9. Oireachtas.ie. (2018). *Dáil Éireann debate - Tuesday, 25 Feb 1986*. [online] Available at: https://www.oireachtas.ie/en/debates/debate/dail/1986-02 25/21/#spk_159 [Accessed 21 Oct. 2018].

Patsy Lawlor

1. 'Colley Attacked by ICA President' *The Irish Times*, Feb 23rd 1978, p.15

2. 'Lip-service To Women' *The Irish Times*, Mar 30th 1981, p.8

3. Interview with Anthony Lawlor, November 2018.

4. Lawlor, Patsy, (1976) "The Three Dimensional Role of Women", Address given at the ICA Summer Council Meeting, Killeshin House, Portlaoise Co. Laois, 14th July 1976. Records of the Irish Countrywomen's Association, NLI MS 39, 349

Bridget Redmond

1. McCarthy, Pat, "We Always Vote Redmond In This House", *The Irish Times*, 12 April, 2018 https://www.irishtimes.com/culture/books/we-always-vote-redmond in-this-house-1.3456897 [Accessed 25 Sept. 2018].

2. Leinster Leader, 10 May 1952 [online] Available at: http://www.kildare.ie/ehistory index.php/funeral-of-bridget-mary-mallick-redmond-1952/ [Accessed 25 Sept. 2018].

3. Oireachtas.ie. (2018). *Dáil Éireann debate - Tuesday, 20 May 1947*. [online] Available at: https://www.oireachtas.ie/en/debates/debate/dail/1947-05-20 speech/333/ [Accessed 25 Sept. 2018].

4. Luddy, Maria, *A 'Sinister and Retrogressive' Proposal: Irish Women's Opposition to the 1937 Draft Constitution in Transactions of the Royal Historical Society*, 15,175-195. [online] Available at http://www.jstor.org/stable/3679367 [Accessed 06 Mar. 2019].

Mary Reynolds
1. Meeting with Noeleen Smith and Mary McKiernan, October 2018.
2. Collins, Stephen, "Hold onto your seat for drama you can count on", *The Irish Times*, 26th February, 2011 [online] Available at:
   https://www.irishtimes.comnews/hold-on-to-your-seat-for-drama-you-can-count-on-1.583203 [Accessed Sept. 2018].
3. Election address from Mrs. M Reynolds, *The Sligo Champion*, 8th May, 1954.

Alice Stopford Green
1. A.S. Green; *Woman's Place in the World of Letters*, Nineteenth Century, June 1897 MacMillan and Co., Limited, London (1913) p.16 [online] Available at:
   https://babel.hathitrust.org/cgi/pt?id=wu.89094823622 [Accessed 22 Jan. 2019].
2. Mitchell, Angus (2006) "Alice Stopford Green and the origins of the African Society", *History Ireland*, 14:4, July/August, 19-24.
3. Oireachtas.ie. (2019). *Seanad Éireann debate - Wednesday, 26 Nov 1924*. [online]
   https://www.oireachtas.ie/en/debates/debate/seanad/1924-11-26/speech/72/ [Accessed 22 Jan. 2019].

Mary Walsh
1. Interview with Vincent Blake
2. Biographical details confirmed by Paddy and Mary O'Toole.
3. Oireachtas.ie. (2019). *Seanad Éireann debate – 4 Feb, 1976* [online] Available at:
   https://www.oireachtas.ie/en/debates/debate/seanad/1976-02-04/3/ [Accessed 7 Oct. 2018].

Jennie Wyse Power
1. Oireachtas.ie. (2018). *Seanad Éireann debate - Thursday, 17 Dec 1925*. [online]
   https://www.oireachtas.ie/en/debates/debate/seanad/1925-12-17/speech/38/ [Accessed 7 Sept. 2018].
2. Oireachtas.ie. (2018). *Seanad Éireann debate - Thursday, 17 Dec 1925*. [online]
   https://www.oireachtas.ie/en/debates/debate/seanad/1925-12-17/speech/46/
3. [Accessed 7 Sept. 2018].
4. McCoole, Sinéad, *No Ordinary Women, Irish Female Activists in the Revolutionary Years 1900 - 1923*. Dublin, The O'Brien Press, 2004.
5. Crampton, C. (2018, 22 October), *The Life of Jennie Wyse Power*, Our Wicklow Heritage: A Community Heritage Archive of County Wicklow [online] Available at:
   http://www.countywicklowheritage.org/page/the_life_of_jenny_wysepower [Accessed 8 Oct. 2018].
6. O'Connor, Sarah; Shepard, Christopher C. (eds.). *Women, Social and Cultural Change in Twentieth Century Ireland*. Cambridge Scholars Publishing.[Accessed 15 August 2018].
7. Oireachtas.ie. (2018). *Seanad Éireann debate - Wednesday, 30 Mar 1927*. [online]
   https://www.oireachtas.ie/en/debates/debate/seanad/1927-03-30/speech/27/ [Accessed 7 Sept. 2018].

SECONDARY SOURCES

Claffey, Úna, *The Women Who Won: Women of the 27th Dáil* Dublin, Attic Press, 1993.

Clancy, Mary, 'Aspects of women's contribution to the Oireachtas debate in the Irish Free State, 1922-1937' in Maria Luddy & Cliona Murphy (eds.), Women Surviving, Dublin, 1990.

Coté, Jane and Dana Hearne Anna Parnell (1852 – 1911) in Mary Cullen and Maria Luddy (eds.), *Women, Power and Consciousness in 19th Century Ireland*, Dublin, Attic Press, 1995.

Cullen-Owens, Rosemary, *Smashing Times A History of the Women's Suffrage Movement 1889-1922*, Dublin, Attic Press, 1984.

Fennell, Nuala, *Political Woman, A Memoir*, Dublin, Currach Press, 2009.

Fitzgerald, Garret, *All In A Life: An Autobiography* Dublin, Gill and Macmillan, 1991.

Fitzgerald, Martina, *Madam Politician, The Women At The Table of Irish Political Power* Dublin, Gill Books, 2018.

Green, A.S., *Woman's Place in the World of Letters*, Nineteenth Century, June 1897 MacMillan and Co., Limited, London, 1913.

Hayes, Alan And Diane Urquhart (eds), *The Irish Women's History Reader*, London, Routledge, 2001.

Hussey, Gemma, *At the Cutting Edge Cabinet Diaries 1982-87*, Dublin, Gill and MacMillan, 1990.

Hussey, Gemma, *Ireland Today: Anatomy of a Changing State*, Dublin, Town House, 1993.

Lee, J.J, *Ireland 1912 – 1985: Politics and Society*, Cambridge, Cambridge University Press, 1989.

Levine, June, *Sisters*, Dublin, Ward River Press, 1982.

Luddy, Maria, 'A 'Sinister and Retrogressive' Proposal: Irish Women's Opposition to the 1937 Draft Constitution' in *Transactions of the Royal Historical Society*, 15, 175-195. 2005

Knirck, Jason, *Women of the Dáil, Gender, Republicanism and the Anglo Irish Treaty*, Dublin, Irish Academic Press, 2006.

Manning, Maurice, *Women in Irish National and Local Politics, 1922-1977*, in Margaret MacCurtain and Donnacha O' Corrain (eds.) *Women in Irish Society: The Historical Dimension*, Dublin, Arlen House, 1978.

Maye, Brian, *Fine Gael, 1923 – 1987*, Dublin, Blackwater Press, 1993.

MacCurtain, Margaret, *Ariadne's Thread – Writing Women into Irish History*, Arlen House, Galway, 2008.

McAuliffe, Mary, *Senator Kathleen A Browne, 1876 – 1943, Patriot, Politician and Practical Farmer*, Tipperary, Roscrea Publications, 2008.

McCoole, Sinéad, *No Ordinary Women, Irish Female Activists in the Revolutionary Years 1900- 1923*, Dublin, The O'Brien Press, 2004.

McGing, Claire, *Women's Political Representation in Dáil Éireann: Revolutionary and Post-Revolutionary Ireland*, Maynooth University, Social Sciences Institute/Department of Geography.

McGuire, James and Quinn, James, *The Dictionary of Irish Biography*, Dublin Royal Irish Academy Cambridge, Cambridge University Press, 2009.

McNamara, Maedhbh and Mooney, Paschal, *Women in Parliament, Ireland 1918–2000*, Dublin, Wolfhound, 2000.

Meehan, Ciara, *The Cosgrave Party: A History of Cumann na nGaedheal, 1923-33*, Dublin, The Royal Irish Academy, 2010.

O'Byrnes, Stephen, *Hiding Behind A Face: Fine Gael Under Fitzgerald*, Dublin, Gill and MacMillan, 1986.

O'Connor, Sarah; Shepard, Christopher C. (eds.). *Women, Social and Cultural Change in Twentieth Century Ireland*. Cambridge Scholars Publishing. Retrieved 15th August 2018.

O'Sullivan, Donal, *The Irish Free State and its Senate: A Study in Contemporary Politics*, London, Faber and Faber Limited, 1940. [online] Available at: https://archive.org/details/in.ernet.dli.2015.115100/page/n3

Ryan, Louise and Ward, Margaret, (eds), *Irish Women and the Vote: Becoming Citizens*, Dublin, Irish Academic Press, 2018.

Walker, Brian M., *Parliamentary Election Results in Ireland, 1918-92 Irish elections to parliaments and parliamentary assemblies at Westminster, Belfast, Dublin, Strasbourg*, Dublin Royal Irish Academy, 1992.

Ward, Margaret, *Unmanageable Revolutionaries*, Kerry, Brandon Book Publishers, 1983.

INDEX

8th Amendment. See Eighth Amendment
Abortion, 9, 61, 70, 71, 74, 78, 79, 86, 90, 106, 125
ADAPT, 68
African Society, 24
Agricultural Policy, 39
Agriculture, 33, 34, 39, 41, 42, 46
Ahearn, Theresa, 118, 119, 120
American Centre For Missing and Abducted Children, 117
Ancient Order Of Hibernians, 106
Andrews, Niall, 83
Arms Crisis, 85
Arnold, Mavis, 94
Arts Council, 101
Association of European Parliamentarians with Africa, 93
Attorney General, 61, 95, 133
Banotti, Mary, 7, 29, 81, 115
Barnes, Monica, 9, 61, 66, 81, 82, 104, 105, 106, 107, 124, 129, 136
Barrett, Sean, 64
Barry, Myra, 7, 8, 63, 66
Belton, Paddy, 78, 111
Birth Control. See Contraception
Blueshirts, The, 33
Bodkin Costello, Dr Thomas, 19
Boer War, 24
Boland, John, 111
Bolger, David, 89
Bolger, Deirdre, 7, 89
Boundary Commission, 14
British Veterinary Association, 110
Browne, Kathleen, 20, 24, 32, 33, 34, 35
Brussels, 83, 90, 112
Bruton, John, 83
Bulbulia, Katharine, 7, 8, 61, 93
Bureau Of Military History, 20
Burke, James, 52
Burke, Joan, 6, 51, 52, 53
Burke, Liam, 64
Burke, Ray, 124
Byrne, Gay, 116, 125
Byrne, J.J., 29, 30
Camogie, 94
Capital Punishment, 90, 98
Carey, Donal, 74
CARI, 77
Carroll, Judge Mella, 132
Casement, Roger, 23, 24
Censorship Of Publications Bill, 27
Chadwick, Edward, 29
Charleton Tribunal. See Disclosure's Tribunal
Charleton, Judge Peter, 131, 134
Child Abduction, 117
Childcare, 79, 133

Children's Care And Protection Bill, 86
Children's Referendum, 131, 133
Children's Rights, 8, 132
Children's Allowance, 60
Citizen's Assembly, 65
Citizenship Rights, 14, 69
Civil Service Amendment Act, 28
Civil Service Regulation Bill, 20
Civil War, 20, 34, 37, 64
Claffey, Úna, 119
Clinton, Mark, 90
Colley, George, 51, 100
Collins, Eddie, 94, 95
Collins, Michael, 23, 27, 29, 81, 115
Collins-O'Driscoll, Margaret, 6, 26, 27, 28, 29, 37, 81, 115
Combat Poverty Agency, 87
Comyn, Michael, 34
Conditions Of Employment Bill, 35
Constitution, 5, 14, 21, 41, 65, 68, 86, 92, 120, 121, 133
Contraception, 8, 68, 70, 86, 100, 106
Cosgrave, W. T., 6, 14
Costello, Declan, 63
Costello, Eileen, 5, 19, 20, 21
Costigan, Mark, 83
Council For The Status Of Women, 105
Craig, James, 16, 17, 29, 30
Crèche, 48, 65
Criminal Assets Bureau, 83
Criminal Justice Bill, 101
Cumann na mBan, 13, 14, 33, 34
Cumann na nGaedheal, 2, 4, 5, 6, 8, 13, 14, 23, 27, 33, 34, 37, 40, 41, 46, 136
Cumann na Saoirse, 5, 13, 14, 15, 19, 20, 23, 33, 34
D'Arcy, Michael, 110, 112
Deasy, Austin, 94, 95
Deserted Wives, 68, 87
Desmond, Eileen, 77, 78
Development Aid, 78, 79, 83,
Dillon, James, 7, 89
Disclosures Tribunal, 131
Discrimination, 13, 47, 48, 49, 51, 68, 106, 120
Divorce, 61, 74, 75, 86, 95, 98, 106, 124
Doherty, Sean, 60
Dooge, James, 55, 98
Dooge, Jim. See Dooge, James
Doyle, Avril, 8, 66, 110
Dublin Christian Citizens' Council, 17
Dukes, Alan, 101
Easter Proclamation, 6, 13
Easter Rising, 13, 23
Economic Strategy, 119
Education, 8, 9, 29, 41, 42, 43, 46, 47, 48, 55, 59, 60, 68, 73, 78, 86, 98, 99, 101, 128, 129
Egan, Dan, 78, 98
Eighth Amendment, 65, 95, 106, 116
Emigration, 39

Emissions Trading Directive, 110, 112
Employment, 21, 35, 39, 43, 47, 48, 49, 52, 65, 86, 87
Enterprise, 102, 119, 131
Equal Pay, 47, 49, 68
Equality, 4, 5, 6, 8, 9, 14, 27, 68, 69, 105, 119, 120, 121, 123, 124, 131, 132, 133, 134
Equestrian Federation of Ireland, 110
Europe, 3, 4, 5, 25, 59, 68, 69, 73, 79, 89, 90, 92, 97, 102, 106, 108, 110, 112, 115, 116, 117
European Association of Former Parliamentarians, 68, 69
European Parliament, 4, 5, 89, 106, 110, 112, 115, 116, 117, 131
European People's Party, 110
European Union Of Young Christian Democrats, 97
Family Law, 68, 69
Family Mediation Service, 69
Family, 69, 70, 71, 78, 79, 81, 83, 86, 87, 89, 90, 91, 94, 99, 101, 102, 107, 111, 115, 116, 123, 124, 125, 126, 132, 133,
Farage, Nigel, 113
Farmer's Rights, 33
Feminist, 7, 59, 97, 124
Fennell, Nuala, 9, 61, 66, 68, 69, 70, 74, 81, 129
Fianna Fáil, 7, 8, 9, 14, 34, 38, 39, 51, 52, 63, 64, 74, 75, 78, 95, 123, 124, 127
Finance Bill, 42, 51
Fitzgerald, Alexis, 77
Fitzgerald, Frances, 2, 4, 7, 9, 123, 131, 136,
Fitzgerald, Garret, 7, 59, 63, 69, 75, 77, 93, 94, 95, 97, 110, 112, 119, 120, 132
Fitzgerald, Mark, 132
Flaherty, Mary, 7, 8, 66, 76, 77, 78
Food Subsidies, 60
Foot and Mouth Disease, 112
Foreign Affairs, 73, 81, 98, 119
Free State, 5, 14, 21, 34
Gaelic League, 13, 19, 33
Gardiner, Dr Frances, 107
Garment Workers' Union, 86
Gender, 2, 4, 5, 6, 8, 9, 14, 34, 48, 60, 65, 133, 136, 137
Geoghegan-Quinn, Máire, 106, 108
Glenn, Alice, 61, 66, 75, 84, 85, 86, 87
Good Friday Agreement, 89, 90
Griffith, Arthur, 19
Guerin, Veronica, 83
Harney, Mary, 93, 95, 123, 124
Haughey, Charles, 60, 64, 85,
Haughey, Charlie. See Haughey, Charles
Health, 21, 23, 46, 60, 68, 69, 70, 71, 75, 77, 78, 81, 85, 86, 89, 99, 101, 112, 125, 127, 132
Healy, John, 95
Higgins, Jim, 73
Higgins, Michael D., 83
Hogan, Patrick, 46
Hogan, Phil, 133
Hogan-O'Higgins, Brigid, 46, 47
Homosexuality, 82, 106

Howlin, Brendan, 112
Howth Gun Running, 23
Hugh Lane Gallery, 78
Hussey, Gemma, 7, 8, 9, 59, 66, 81, 93, 98, 129
Hyde, Douglas, 19
Illegitimacy, 8, 63, 69, 74, 78, 96, 97, 98
Income Tax Act, 51
Independent, 5, 14, 42, 59, 69, 86, 102, 113, 120
Inghinidhe na hÉireann, 13
Institute Of Veterinary and Agricultural Science, 39
Irish Countrywomen's Association, 33, 34, 100, 102
Irish Creamery Milk Supplier Association, 127
Irish Literary Society, 19
Irish National Land League, 13, 33
Irish Parliamentary Society, 69
Irish Volunteers, The, 33
Irish Widows Association, 51
Irish Women's Franchise League, 13
Irish Women's Liberation Movement, 68, 115
Jackman, Mary, 7, 8, 126, 127
Juries, 14, 16, 17, 20, 28, 52, 55, 56
Justice, 60, 68, 73, 81, 83, 101, 115, 121, 123, 124, 131, 133, 134
Kearney, Miriam, 7, 8, 97
Kennedy, Geraldine, 124
Kennedy, John F., 115
Kenny, Mary, 68
Keogh, Helen, 8, 123
Kilmainham Gaol, 13, 34
Kingsley, Mary, 24
Labour Party, 7, 8, 35, 77, 78, 79, 95, 107, 110
Ladies' Land League, 2, 6, 13, 33
Land Rehabilitation Scheme, 39
Late Late Show, 116, 125
Lawlor, Patsy, 90, 100, 101, 102
Leinster House, 38, 47, 60, 61, 112
Lisbon Treaty, 113
Live Aid, 83
Local Government (Ireland) Act, 5
Lynch, Jack, 63, 64
Macra na Feirme, 120
Malahide Mosquito, 81
Manning, Maurice, 95
Marital Rape, 8, 60
Marriage Equality, 8, 131, 133
Married Persons Tax Reform Association, 51, 100
Maternity, 65, 69
McAleese, Mary, 115
McCabe, Jerry, 83
McCreevy, Charlie, 63
McGuinness, Catherine, 98
McGuinness, Mairead, 112
McManus, Liz, 125
Merkel, Angela, 108
Minister For Agriculture, 46
Minister for Business, Enterprise and Innovation, 131

143

Minister for Children And Youth Affairs, 131
Minister for Children, 131, 133
Minister for Education, 8, 42, 59, 60
Minister for Finance, 51, 52, 100
Minister for Foreign Affairs, 98
Minister for Health, 60, 70
Minister for Justice, 60, 81, 83, 115, 131, 133
Minister for Labour, 59
Minister for Social Welfare, 59
Minister for Women's Affairs, 59
Minister of State, 68, 69, 77, 110, 111
Mitchell, Gay, 120
Mitchell, Jim, 60, 132
Moravio, Alberto, 116
National Childbirth Trust, 132
National Economic And Social Forum, 73
National Forum For Europe, 73
National University of Ireland, 59
National Women's Council, 131
Northern Ireland, 85, 97, 98
O'Donoghue, John, 83
Office of Public Works, 110, 111
O'Higgins, Michael, 46
Oireachtas Women, 125
O'Leary, Sean, 98
O'Malley, Dessie, 95
OPW. See Office of Public Works
O'Reilly, Eddie, 112
O'Rourke, Mary, 9, 60
Owen, Nora, 9, 29, 66, 79, 81, 115
Paisley, Ian, 117
Parnell, Charles Stewart, 13
PDs. See Progressive Democrats
Pensions, 8, 53, 79
Postnatal Depression, 105
Poverty, 74, 78, 86, 87
Pratt, Hilary, 93
Prendergast, Peter, 74, 78, 81, 94
Presidential Election, 115
Progressive Democrats, 93, 123
Quotas, 61, 65, 95, 110, 113, 125, 133
Racecourses Bill, 41
Redmond, Bridget Mary, 41,
Redmond, John, 41
Redmond, William (Willie), 41
Refuge, 8, 68, 94, 116, 117
Representation of Women, 100
Reynolds, Gerry, 38
Reynolds, Mary, 6, 36, 37, 38, 39
Reynolds, Paddy, 37, 38
Reynolds, Patrick J., 38
Robinson, Mary, 61, 98, 106
Rock, Noel, 79
Rural Affairs, 33
Rural Development, 119
Russell, Ted, 128
Rutland Centre, 115, 117

Ryan, Jim, 34
Sexual Abuse, 124
Sexual Offences Act, 133
Shatter, Alan, 82
Single Parents, 87
Sinn Féin, 13, 19, 20, 33, 34, 73
Social Welfare, 48, 49, 53, 55, 59, 60, 77, 78, 79, 99, 101
Society for the Protection of Unborn Children, SPUC, 74, 90
St Patrick's Day Parade, 106
St Patrick's Institute, 133
St Vincent de Paul, 46
Stack, Austin, 20
Stopford Green, Alice, 22, 23, 24, 34
Strasbourg, 113
Suffragettes, 107
Sutherland, Peter, 61, 65, 82, 95, 116
Tánaiste, 2, 3, 93, 131, 133
Taoiseach, 64, 68, 69, 77, 97, 98, 110, 112
Tax Allowance, 82
Taylor, Frank, 73
Taylor, Mervyn, 124
Taylor-Quinn, Madeleine 7, 8, 66, 73, 129
Tipperary Rural Business Development Institute, 119
Travellers, 124
UKIP, 113
Unemployment, 48, 49, 52, 65, 87
Vaccination, 29, 30
Veterinary Medicines Directive, 112
Vocational Education Committee, 55, 101
Walsh, Mary, 55, 56,
War of Independence, 20
Wearing of Uniforms Restrictions Bill, 34
Webb, Beatrice, 24
Widows, 51, 52, 53, 68, 81, 100
Women Elect, 3, 8, 105, 107, 108, 136
Women's Aid, 68, 69, 115, 116
Women's Council. See National Women's Council
Women's Political Association, 8, 58, 59, 60, 61, 69, 78, 93, 105, 106, 122, 123, 125, 132
Women's Rights, 7, 9, 14, 63, 68, 69, 73, 74, 79, 81, 85, 105, 106, 108, 120, 121, 123, 126, 131
Women's Libbers, 49, 85
Wood Quay, 77, 78
World Anti-Communist League, 85
World Vision, 123
WPA. See Women's Political Association
Wyse Power, Jane 'Jennie', 2, 6, 12, 13, 14, 16, 20, 27
Yeats, W.B., 19
Young Fine Gael, 7, 8, 62, 63, 65, 73, 74, 76, 78, 84, 97, 98, 99

THE AUTHORS

Maria Hegarty is a researcher and equality campaigner who works to promote diversity and inclusion. She studied Business, Economics and Social Studies at Trinity College Dublin and is the Founder of Equality Strategies Ltd and Diversity Charter Ireland.

Martina Murray is a writer and historian with a particular interest in campaigns around social change. She studied English and History at Trinity College Dublin and currently works as a freelance writer and web editor.

Women have been active in political parties since before the foundation of the state, yet very little is known about female politicians or their achievements. The current era of state centenary celebrations offers a timely opportunity to address this gap, and to hear from those women who served as public representatives both nationally and in Europe.

Proud to Serve uncovers the achievements of twenty-eight women who had successful political careers with Cumann na nGaedheal and Fine Gael. Their voices are presented chronologically, in order of the date of their first election or appointment to the Seanad, Dáil and European Parliament, between the years 1922 and 1992.

In bringing together the political reflections and accomplishments of these female politicians for the first time, *Proud to Serve* gives voice to the experiences of an extraordinary group of women. Each made important contributions to Irish politics and balanced many competing demands at a time when women's participation in public life was particularly challenging.

This volume tells us something of their personal and political backgrounds, their experience of political life and the issues that were prevalent during their time in politics. In highlighting the contribution and achievements of this remarkable group of women, the book aims to stimulate broader awareness and debate about the role and work of women in Irish political life.

FINE GAEL ★

www.finegael.ie